Drawing Near

W9-BVL-177

Drawing Near

Drawing Near

with

Daily Bible Reading
and Prayer

by

Kenneth Boa and Max Anders

Thomas Nelson Publishers
Nashville

This special Billy Graham Evangelistic
Association edition is published with permission
from Thomas Nelson Publishers.

Drawing Near
Copyright © 1987 by Kenneth Boa and Max Anders

All Scripture quotations are from or based upon:

The Holy Bible, New King James Version
Copyright © 1982 by Thomas Nelson, Inc.

The New King James Bible, New Testament
Copyright © 1979 by Thomas Nelson, Inc.
The New King James Bible, New Testament and Psalms
Copyright © 1980 by Thomas Nelson, Inc.

Published in Nashville, Tennessee, by Thomas Nelson, Inc.,
and distributed in Canada by Lawson Falle, Ltd., Cambridge, Ontario.

ISBN: 0-913367-10-9

All rights reserved.
Printed in the United States of America

"Draw near to God and He will draw near to you."

(James 4:8)

Dedication

To our wives, Karen and Margie,
for whom this was a labor of love.

Acknowledgments

Ken would like to thank the staff of Search Ministries for their encouragement and supportiveness during the writing of this project. Special thanks go to Larry Moody, David Krueger, Ed Diaz, Rod MacIlvaine, John Rayls, and Bob Shelley, and to Bob Hendricks for the outline "loving God completely, loving self correctly, loving others compassionately" in the Memory Verse Guide.

Max would like to thank the people of Grace Community Church for their inestimable contribution to his life as he was working on this material.

Both of us would like to acknowledge a life-changing contribution made by the *Private Devotions* of Lancelot Andrewes, a seventeenth-century Anglican bishop and major translator of the King James Bible.

Contents

Introduction

Drawing Near is a special book. Its purpose is to help you enrich two key areas of Christian devotion: consistent and effective prayer, and knowledge of the Bible. To fulfill that purpose, the book is divided into three parts.

PART I

Part I is a topical arrangement of Bible passages. These Scriptures are grouped together as they relate to various aspects of Christian prayer life:

> Prayers of Adoration,
> Prayers for Forgiveness,
> Prayers for Renewal,
> Prayers for Personal Needs,
> Prayers for Others,
> Prayers of Affirmation,
> Prayers of Thanksgiving,
> Closing Prayers.

The Scriptures have been slightly edited so that, as you read them, they become your personal prayers. You can actually pray Scripture back to God! This section of *Drawing Near* is a complete set of biblical prayers which you can use as a support to your prayer life, giving it breadth and depth. A combination of these aspects of prayer will give you a "balanced diet" for your prayer life.

Become familiar with the topical arrangement of Bible prayers. Learn to incorporate Scriptures from each section into your prayer life. When used on a regular basis, these Scriptures will plant biblical truth within your heart and mind.

Thus, the Bible itself becomes a guide to one of the most elusive goals of Christian devotion, a faithful and effective prayer life. With this book, you will no longer have to feel guilty and helpless about a weak prayer life; now you can do something about it. And since the prayers are all from the Bible, you can be sure these are prayers God would want you to pray.

PART II

The purpose of Part II is to encourage and guide your reading of Scripture. It contains two keys which open up the joys of your Christian life: a guide to Bible reading and a guide to Bible memory.

Drawing Near gives you ten ways to read through the Bible. Choose one or more of the methods of Bible reading. Be flexible. Feel free to change methods or combinations of methods as you desire. You may choose to integrate one method or combination with your daily prayer time and to use another method or combination at another time of day. The important thing is to choose a system that works for you. Then make a personal commitment to read the Bible every day.

There is no more effective way to transform and renew your mind (Rom. 12:1, 2) than by memorizing and meditating upon Scripture. Memorization places Scripture at your fingertips, always at your disposal for use on unexpected occasions. To guide you in Bible memory, three levels are given on which to memorize important Bible verses:

1. ten major areas of the Christian walk,

2. themes of loving God, self, and others, and
3. ten areas of Christian doctrine.

PART III

Part III draws from Parts I and II and develops a thirty-one-day pattern for devotional prayer, Bible reading, and Bible memory. For each day, Scriptures are selected from the aspects of prayer found in Part I. By careful arrangement, *Drawing Near* leads you through a time of rich devotion, starting with Bible reading. Then, with the heavenly light of Scripture, enter into a time of praise and adoration of God, personal confessions, prayers for self and others, concluding with affirmations and thanksgivings to God. Within this daily pattern for prayer, take opportunities to express your individual concerns and spontaneous prayers. In closing each day's prayer time, select and memorize the Bible verse of your choosing.

You will find that *Drawing Near* offers two major benefits: a guide to a consistent and effective prayer life, and a guide to daily Bible reading and memorization. Its usefulness is great, the applications are many. And since the book contains a topical arrangement of prayers along with several Bible reading and Bible memory plans, you can develop your devotional time with infinite variety. *Drawing Near* will prove useful for many years.

"Draw near to God and He will draw near to you."
(James 4:8)

Part I
A Topical Arrangement
of Scriptural Prayers

Eight Prayer Principles
From
The Lord's Prayer

Communication, communion, and spiritual intimacy
with God are things we all long for. They are part of
the new birth . . . part of our new relationship with
Him. The desire to pray comes from deep within the
regenerate heart. Yet when we kneel to pray, we often
feel a sense of inadequacy and uncertainty. How do
we pray? For what do we pray? This sense of
inadequacy is as old as the Bible itself. Jesus'
disciples came to Him while He was praying and
said, "Lord, teach us to pray, as John also taught his
disciples." In response, Jesus instructed His
disciples in prayer. As we look closely at His model
prayer, we can see eight principles that should always
guide our prayers: Adoration, Thanksgiving,
Affirmation, Forgiveness, Renewal, Personal Needs,
Others' Needs, and Closing Prayers.

"HALLOWED BE YOUR NAME." The first
principle is the principle of praise. Jesus began
His prayer by offering honor to the One to whom
He was praying. From other passages in
Scripture, we learn that the concept of praise
includes ADORATION, honoring God for who He
is, and THANKSGIVING, honoring Him for
what He has done.

"YOUR KINGDOM COME. YOUR WILL BE
DONE." The second principle is the principle of

AFFIRMATION, that is, agreeing with the will of God, and submitting ourselves to it. To affirm the revealed will of God is to align ourselves with it in sincere obedience from the heart.

"GIVE US THIS DAY OUR DAILY BREAD." In this phrase is found the principle of supplication, or asking things from God. In Matthew 7, Jesus teaches us to ask, to seek, and to knock, in our life of prayer. As we see this concept expanded in other passages, we note that it is God's gracious offer to encourage us to ask Him concerning PERSONAL NEEDS and OTHERS' NEEDS.

"FORGIVE US OUR DEBTS." FORGIVENESS is the next principle that emerges from the pattern of Jesus' prayer. We are to keep our hearts cleansed from sin by asking for forgiveness for our sins. In this way, the apostle John tells us, we can live lives of fellowship with Him, in unbroken harmony.

"DELIVER US FROM THE EVIL ONE." We constantly face temptation to sin. As we battle to overcome temptation in our lives, prayer for RENEWAL is a continuous need.

"FOR YOURS IS THE KINGDOM AND THE POWER AND THE GLORY FOREVER. AMEN." The final concept is a suitable CLOSING PRAYER, which elevates the Lord and brings our prayers to a close.

There are many passages of Scripture that fall into
these eight categories. The prayers in Part I are
comprised entirely of Scripture, categorized
according to the principles found in the Lord's Prayer.
The authors have rewritten them when necessary in
the first person so that they can be easily prayed
back to the Lord. See the Scripture Prayer Guide
(Part III of this book) for a plan that incorporates
these prayers into a total worship experience.

Prayers of Adoration

Who is like You, O LORD, among the gods?
Who is like You, glorious in holiness,
Fearful in praises, doing wonders?   Ex. 15:11

Thank you, LORD God, that You are merciful and
gracious, longsuffering, and abounding in goodness
and truth, keeping mercy for thousands, forgiving
iniquity and transgression and sin, by no means
clearing the guilty, visiting the iniquity of the fathers
upon the children and the children's children to the
third and the fourth generation.   Ex. 34:6, 7

You are my praise, and You are my God, who have
done for me these great and awesome things which
my eyes have seen.   Deut. 10:21

You are the Rock, Your work is perfect;
For all Your ways are justice,
A God of truth and without injustice;
Righteous and upright are You.   Deut. 32:4

Therefore You are great, O Lord GOD. For there is
none like You, nor is there any God besides You,
according to all that we have heard with our ears.
                                               2 Sam. 7:22

The LORD lives!
Blessed be my Rock!
Let God be exalted,
The Rock of my salvation!   2 Sam. 22:47

LORD God of Israel, there is no God in heaven above
or on earth below like You, who keep Your covenant
and mercy with Your servants who walk before You
with all their hearts.   1 Kin. 8:23

O LORD God of Israel, the One who dwells between
the cherubim, You are God, You alone, of all the
kingdoms of the earth. You have made heaven and
earth.   2 Kin. 19:15

Give to the LORD, O families of the peoples,
Give to the LORD glory and strength.
Give to the LORD the glory due His name;
Bring an offering, and come before Him.
Oh, worship the LORD in the beauty of holiness!
Tremble before Him, all the earth.
                                              1 Chr. 16:28-30

Blessed are You, LORD God of Israel, our Father,
    forever and ever.
Yours, O LORD, is the greatness,
The power and the glory,
The victory and the majesty;
For all that is in heaven and in earth is Yours;
Yours is the kingdom, O LORD,
And You are exalted as head over all.
Both riches and honor come from You,
And You reign over all.
In Your hand it is to make great
And to give strength to all.
Now therefore, our God,
We thank You
And praise Your glorious name.   1 Chr. 29:10-13

O LORD God of our fathers, are You not God in
heaven, and do You not rule over all the kingdoms
of the nations, and in Your hand is there not power
and might, so that no one is able to withstand You?
2 Chr. 20:6

Blessed be Your glorious name,
Which is exalted above all blessing and praise!
You alone are the LORD;
You have made heaven,
The heaven of heavens, with all their host,
The earth and everything on it,
The seas and all that is in them,
And You preserve them all.
The host of heaven worships You.   Neh. 9:5, 6

I will praise the LORD according to His
    righteousness,
And will sing praise to the name of the LORD
    Most High.   Ps. 7:17

O LORD, our Lord,
How excellent is Your name in all the earth,
Who have set Your glory above the heavens!
Ps. 8:1

I will praise You, O LORD with my whole heart;
I will tell of all Your marvelous works.
I will be glad and rejoice in You;
I will sing praise to Your name, O Most High.
Ps. 9:1, 2

I will love You, O LORD, my strength.
The LORD is my rock and my fortress and my
    deliverer;

My God, my strength, in whom I will trust;
My shield and the horn of my salvation, my
    stronghold.
I will call upon the LORD, who is worthy to be
    praised;
So shall I be saved from my enemies.   Ps. 18:1-3

The LORD lives!
Blessed be my Rock!
Let the God of my salvation be exalted.

Ps. 18:46

Be exalted, O LORD, in your own strength!
We will sing and praise Your power.   Ps.21:13

Be glad in the LORD and rejoice, you righteous;
And shout for joy, all you upright in heart!

Ps. 32:11

Rejoice in the LORD, O you righteous!
For praise from the upright is beautiful.   Ps. 33:1

I will bless the LORD at all times;
His praise shall continually be in my mouth.
My soul shall make its boast in the LORD;
The humble shall hear of it and be glad.
Oh, magnify the LORD with me,
And let us exalt His name together.   Ps. 34:1-3

Oh, taste and see that the LORD is good;
Blessed is the man who trusts in Him!
Oh, fear the LORD, you His saints!
There is no want to those who fear Him.

Ps. 34:8, 9

For with You is the fountain of life;
In Your light we see light. Ps. 36:9

Your throne, O God, is forever and ever;
A scepter of righteousness is the scepter of Your
    kingdom.
You love righteousness and hate wickedness;
Therefore God, Your God, has anointed You
With the oil of gladness more than Your companions.
Ps. 45:6, 7

We have thought, O God, on Your lovingkindness,
In the midst of Your temple.
According to Your name, O God,
So is Your praise to the ends of the earth;
Your right hand is full of righteousness.
Ps. 48:9, 10

I will praise You, O Lord, among the peoples;
I will sing to You among the nations.
For Your mercy reaches unto the heavens,
And Your truth unto the clouds.
Be exalted, O God, above the heavens;
Let Your glory be above all the earth.
Ps. 57:9-11

O God, You are my God;
Early will I seek You;
My soul thirsts for You;
My flesh longs for You
In a dry and thirsty land
Where there is no water.
So I have looked for You in the sanctuary,

To see Your power and Your glory.
Because Your lovingkindness is better than life,
My lips shall praise You.
Thus I will bless You while I live;
I will lift up my hands in Your name.
My soul shall be satisfied as with marrow and
    fatness,
And my mouth shall praise You with joyful lips.
When I remember You on my bed,
I meditate on You in the night watches,
Because You have been my help,
Therefore in the shadow of Your wings I will rejoice.

Ps. 63:1-7

Make a joyful shout to God, all the earth!
Sing out the honor of His name;
Make His praise glorious.
Say to God,
"How awesome are Your works!
All the earth shall worship You
And sing praises to You;
They shall sing praises to Your name."   Ps. 66:1-4

Let my mouth be filled with Your praise
And with Your glory all the day.   Ps. 71:8

But I will hope continually,
And will praise You yet more and more.
My mouth shall tell of Your righteousness
And Your salvation all the day,
For I do not know their limits.
I will go in the strength of the Lord GOD;
I will make mention of Your righteousness,
    of Yours only.

O God, You have taught me from my youth;
And to this day I declare Your wondrous works.

Ps. 71:14-17

Blessed be the LORD God, the God of Israel,
Who only does wondrous things!
And blessed be His glorious name forever!
And let the whole earth be filled with His glory.
Amen and Amen.   Ps. 72:18, 19

LORD, You have been our dwelling place in all
      generations.
Before the mountains were brought forth,
Or ever You had formed the earth and the world,
Even from everlasting to everlasting, You are God.

Ps. 90:1, 2

It is good to give thanks to the LORD,
And to sing praises to Your name, O Most High;
To declare Your lovingkindness in the morning,
And Your faithfulness every night.   Ps. 92:1, 2

The LORD reigns,
He is clothed with majesty;
The LORD is clothed,
He has girded Himself with strength.
Surely the world is established, so that it cannot be
      moved.
Your throne is established from of old;
You are from everlasting.   Ps. 93:1, 2

Oh come, let us sing to the LORD!
Let us shout joyfully to the Rock of our salvation.

Let us come before His presence with thanksgiving;
Let us shout joyfully to Him with psalms.
For the LORD is the great God,
And the great King above all gods.
Oh come, let us worship and bow down;
Let us kneel before the LORD our Maker.
For He is our God,
And we are the people of His pasture,
And the sheep of His hand.   Ps. 95:1-3, 6, 7

Oh, sing to the LORD a new song!
Sing to the LORD, all the earth.
Sing to the LORD, bless His name;
Proclaim good news of His salvation from day to day.
Declare His glory among the nations,
His wonders among all peoples.
For the LORD is great and greatly to be praised;
He is to be feared above all gods.
For all the gods of the peoples are idols,
But the LORD made the heavens.
Honor and majesty are before Him;
Strength and beauty are in His sanctuary.
                                        Ps. 96:1-6

You who love the LORD, hate evil!
He preserves the souls of His saints;
He delivers them out of the hand of the wicked.
Light is sown for the righteous,
And gladness for the upright in heart.
Rejoice in the LORD, you righteous,
And give thanks at the remembrance of His holy
     name.   Ps. 97:10-12

Make a joyful shout to the LORD, all you lands!
Serve the LORD with gladness;
Come before His presence with singing.
Know that the LORD, He is God;
It is He who has made us, and not we ourselves;
We are His people and the sheep of His pasture.
Enter into His gates with thanksgiving,
And into His courts with praise.
Be thankful to Him, and bless His name.
For the LORD is good;
His mercy is everlasting,
And His truth endures to all generations.

Ps. 100:1-5

Bless the LORD, O my soul!
O LORD my God, You are very great:
You are clothed with honor and majesty,
Who cover Yourself with light as with a garment,
Who stretch out the heavens like a curtain.

Ps. 104:1, 2

O LORD, how manifold are Your works!
In wisdom You have made them all.
The earth is full of Your possessions.   Ps. 104:24

May the glory of the LORD endure forever;
May the LORD rejoice in His works.   Ps. 104:31

I will sing to the LORD as long as I live;
I will sing praise to my God while I have my being.
May my meditation be sweet to Him;
I will be glad in the LORD.   Ps. 104:33, 34

Oh, give thanks to the LORD!
Call upon His name;
Make known His deeds among the peoples!
Sing to Him, sing psalms to Him;
Talk of all His wondrous works!
Glory in His holy name;
Let the hearts of those rejoice who seek the LORD!
Seek the LORD and His strength;
Seek His face evermore!
Remember His marvelous works which He has done,
His wonders, and the judgments of His mouth.

Ps. 105:1-5

Praise the LORD!
Oh, give thanks to the LORD, for He is good!
For His mercy endures forever.
Who can utter the mighty acts of the LORD?
Who can declare all His praise?   Ps. 106:1, 2

O God, my heart is steadfast;
I will sing and give praise, even with my glory.
Awake, lute and harp!
I will awaken the dawn.
I will praise You, O LORD, among the peoples,
And I will sing praises to You among the nations.
For Your mercy is great above the heavens,
And Your truth reaches to the clouds.
Be exalted, O God, above the heavens,
And Your glory above all the earth.   Ps.108:1-5

Praise the LORD!
Blessed is the man who fears You,
Who delights greatly in Your commandments.

Ps. 112:1

Praise the LORD!
Praise, O servants of the LORD,
Praise the name of the LORD!
Blessed be the name of the LORD
From this time forth and forevermore!
From the rising of the sun to its going down
The LORD's name is to be praised.
The LORD is high above all nations,
His glory above the heavens.
Who is like the LORD our God,
Who dwells on high,
Who humbles Himself to behold
The things that are in the heavens and in the earth?

Ps. 113:1-6

Not unto us, O LORD, not unto us,
But to Your name give glory,
Because of Your mercy,
Because of Your truth.   Ps. 115:1

Forever, O LORD,
Your word is settled in heaven.
Your faithfulness endures to all generations;
You established the earth, and it abides.

Ps. 119:89, 90

Unto You I lift up my eyes,
O You who dwell in the heavens.
Behold, as the eyes of servants look to the hand of
    their masters,
As the eyes of a maid to the hand of her mistress,
So our eyes look to You our God,
Until You have mercy on us.   Ps. 123:1, 2

For I know that You are great,
And You are above all gods.
Whatever You please You do,
In heaven and in earth,
In the seas and in all deep places.   Ps. 135:5, 6

I will praise You, for I am fearfully and wonderfully
     made;
Marvelous are Your works,
And that my soul knows very well.   Ps. 139:14

I will extol You, my God, O King;
And I will bless Your name forever and ever.
Every day I will bless You,
And I will praise Your name forever and ever.
Great is the LORD, and greatly to be praised;
And His greatness is unsearchable.
One generation shall praise Your works to another,
And shall declare Your mighty acts.
I will meditate on the glorious splendor of Your
     majesty,
And on Your wondrous works.
Men shall speak of the might of Your awesome acts,
And I will declare Your greatness.
They shall utter the memory of Your great goodness,
And shall sing of Your righteousness.
The LORD is gracious and full of compassion,
Slow to anger and great in mercy.
The LORD is good to all,
And His tender mercies are over all His works.
                              Ps. 145:1-9

All Your works shall praise You, O LORD,
And Your saints shall bless You.
They shall speak of the glory of Your kingdom,
And talk of Your power,
To make known to the sons of men His mighty acts,
And the glorious majesty of His kingdom.
Your kingdom is an everlasting kingdom,
And Your dominion endures throughout all
    generations.   Ps. 145:10-13

The LORD is righteous in all His ways,
Gracious in all His works.
The LORD is near to all who call upon Him,
To all who call upon Him in truth.
He will fulfill the desire of those who fear Him;
He also will hear their cry and save them.
My mouth shall speak the praise of the LORD,
And all flesh shall bless His holy name
Forever and ever.   Ps. 145:17-19, 21

Praise the LORD!
Praise the LORD, O my soul!
While I live I will praise You;
I will sing praises to You while I have my being.
                          Ps. 146:1, 2

Praise the LORD!
For it is good to sing praises to our God;
For it is pleasant, and praise is beautiful.
                          Ps. 147:1

Praise the LORD!
Praise God in His sanctuary;

Praise Him in His mighty firmament!
Praise Him for His mighty acts;
Praise Him according to His excellent greatness!
Praise Him with the sound of the trumpet;
Praise Him with the lute and harp!
Praise Him with the timbrel and dance;
Praise Him with stringed instruments and flutes!
Praise Him with loud cymbals;
Praise Him with clashing cymbals!
Let everything that has breath praise the LORD.
Praise the LORD!   Ps. 150:1-6

Holy, holy, holy is the LORD of hosts;
The whole earth is full of His glory!   Is. 6:3

Inasmuch as there is none like You, O LORD
(You are great, and Your name is great in might),
Who would not fear You, O King of the nations?
For this is Your rightful due,
For among all the wise men of the nations,
And in all their kingdoms,
There is none like You.   Jer. 10:6, 7

Ah, Lord GOD! Behold, You have made the heavens
and the earth by Your great power and outstretched
arm. There is nothing too hard for You. You show
lovingkindness to thousands, and repay the iniquity
of the fathers into the bosom of their children after
them—the Great, the Mighty God, whose name is
the LORD of hosts. You are great in counsel and
mighty in work, for your eyes are open to all the ways
of the sons of men, to give everyone according to his
ways and according to the fruit of his doings.
                                                         Jer. 32:17-19

31

You, O LORD, remain forever,
Your throne from generation to generation.

Lam. 5:19

Blessed be the name of God forever and ever,
For wisdom and might are His.
And He changes the times and the seasons;
He removes kings and raises up kings;
He gives wisdom to the wise
And knowledge to those who have understanding.
He reveals deep and secret things;
He knows what is in the darkness,
And light dwells with Him.

Dan. 2:20-22

Hosanna to the Son of David!
Blessed is He who comes in the name of the LORD!
Hosanna in the highest!

Matt. 21:9

My soul magnifies You,
And my spirit has rejoiced in You my Savior.

Luke 1:46, 47

You who are mighty have done great things for me,
And holy is Your name.
And Your mercy is on those who fear You
From generation to generation.

Luke 1:49, 50

Glory to God in the highest,
And on earth peace, goodwill toward men!

Luke 2:14

Oh, the depth of the riches both of the wisdom and
knowledge of God! How unsearchable are His
judgments and His ways past finding out!

Rom. 11:33

Blessed are You the God and Father of our Lord
Jesus Christ, who have blessed us with every
spiritual blessing in the heavenly places in Christ.

Eph. 1:3

Holy, holy, holy,
Lord God Almighty,
Who was and is and is to come!   Rev. 4:8

You are worthy, O Lord,
To receive glory and honor and power;
For You created all things,
And by Your will they exist and were created.

Rev. 4:11

You are worthy to take the scroll,
And to open its seals;
For You were slain,
And have redeemed us to God by Your blood
Out of every tribe and tongue and people and nation,
And have made us kings and priests to our God;
And we shall reign on the earth.   Rev. 5:9, 10

Worthy is the Lamb who was slain
To receive power and riches and wisdom,
And strength and honor and glory and blessing!

Rev. 5:12

Great and marvelous are Your works,
Lord God Almighty!
Just and true are Your ways,
O King of the saints!
Who shall not fear You, O Lord, and glorify Your
    name?

For You alone are holy.
For all nations shall come and worship before You,
For Your judgments have been manifested.

Rev. 15:3, 4

Alleluia! Salvation and glory and honor and power to
You our God!

Rev. 19:1

Praise You, all we Your servants and those who fear
You, both small and great!

Rev. 19:5

You are the Root and the Offspring of David, the
Bright and Morning Star.

Rev. 22:16

Prayers for Forgiveness

Oh, my lord! Please do not lay this sin on us, in
which we have done foolishly and in which we have
sinned.

Num. 12:11

Forgive us, Lord, when we are unmindful of the Rock
    who begot us,
And forget the God who fathered us.

Deut. 32:18

Indeed I have sinned against the LORD God of Israel.

Josh. 7:20

Has the LORD as great delight in burnt offerings and
    sacrifices,
As in obeying the voice of the LORD?
Behold, to obey is better than sacrifice,
And to heed than the fat of rams.

1 Sam. 15:22

For the LORD does not see as man sees; for man looks at the outward appearance, but the LORD looks at the heart.   1 Sam. 16:7

I have sinned greatly in what I have done; but now, I pray, O LORD, take away the iniquity of Your servant, for I have done very foolishly.   2 Sam. 24:10

O my God, I am too ashamed and humiliated to lift up my face to You, my God; for our iniquities have risen higher than our heads, and our guilt has grown up to the heavens.   Ezra 9:6

LORD God of heaven, O great and awesome God, You who keep Your covenant and mercy with those who love You and observe Your commandments, please let Your ear be attentive and Your eyes open, that You may hear the prayer of Your servant which I pray before You now, day and night, for the children of Israel your servants, and confess the sins of the children of Israel which we have sinned against You. Both my father's house and I have sinned.
                    Neh. 1:5, 6

You are just in all that has befallen us;
For You have dealt faithfully,
But we have done wickedly.   Neh. 9:33

What is man, that You should exalt him,
That You should set Your heart on him,
That You should visit him every morning,
And test him every moment?   Job 7:17, 18

God is wise in heart and mighty in strength.
Who has hardened himself against Him and
    prospered?   Job 9:4

You know the way that I take;
When You have tested me, I shall come forth as gold.
                                  Job 23:10

I have heard of You by the hearing of the ear,
But now my eye sees You.
Therefore I abhor myself,
And repent in dust and ashes.   Job 42:5, 6

For You are not a God who takes pleasure in
    wickedness,
Nor shall evil dwell with You.   Ps. 5:4

O LORD, do not rebuke me in Your anger,
Nor chasten me in Your hot displeasure.
Have mercy on me, O LORD, for I am weak;
O LORD, heal me, for my bones are troubled.
My soul also is greatly troubled.   Ps. 6:1-3

Who can understand his errors?
Cleanse me from secret faults.
Keep back Your servant also from presumptuous
    sins;
Let them not have dominion over me.
Then I shall be blameless,
And I shall be innocent of great transgression.
                            Ps. 19:12, 13

Remember, O LORD, Your tender mercies and Your
    lovingkindnesses,

For they are from of old.
Do not remember the sins of my youth, nor my
     transgressions;
According to Your mercy remember me,
For Your goodness' sake, O LORD.
Good and upright is the LORD;
Therefore He teaches sinners in the way.
The humble He guides in justice,
And the humble He teaches His way.
All the paths of the LORD are mercy and truth,
To such as keep His covenant and His testimonies.
For Your name's sake, O LORD,
Pardon my iniquity, for it is great.   Ps. 25:6-11

Sing praise to the LORD, you saints of His,
And give thanks at the remembrance of His holy
     name.
For His anger is but for a moment,
His favor is for life;
Weeping may endure for a night,
But joy comes in the morning.   Ps. 30:4, 5

Blessed is he whose transgression is forgiven,
Whose sin is covered.
Blessed is the man to whom the LORD does not
     impute iniquity,
And in whose spirit there is no deceit.
When I kept silent, my bones grew old
Through my groaning all the day long.
For day and night Your hand was heavy upon me;
My vitality was turned into the drought of summer.
I acknowledged my sin to You,
And my iniquity I have not hidden.

37

I said, "I will confess my transgressions to the
    LORD,"
And You forgave the iniquity of my sin.

Ps. 32:1-5

The LORD is near to those who have a broken heart,
And saves such as have a contrite spirit.

Ps. 34:18

LORD, be merciful to me;
Heal my soul, for I have sinned against You.

Ps. 41:4

Have mercy upon me, O God,
According to Your lovingkindness;
According to the multitude of Your tender mercies,
Blot out my transgressions.
Wash me thoroughly from my iniquity,
And cleanse me from my sin.
For I acknowledge my transgressions,
And my sin is always before me.
Against You, You only, have I sinned,
And done this evil in Your sight—
That You may be found just when You speak,
And blameless when You judge.   Ps. 51:1-4

Purge me with hyssop, and I shall be clean;
Wash me, and I shall be whiter than snow.
Make me hear joy and gladness,
That the bones You have broken may rejoice.
Hide Your face from my sins,
And blot out all my iniquities.
Create in me a clean heart, O God,

38

And renew a steadfast spirit within me.
Do not cast me away from Your presence,
And do not take Your Holy Spirit from me.
Restore to me the joy of Your salvation,
And uphold me by Your generous Spirit.
Then I will teach transgressors Your ways,
And sinners shall be converted to You.

Ps. 51:7-13

Deliver me from the guilt of bloodshed, O God,
The God of my salvation,
And my tongue shall sing aloud of Your
    righteousness.
O Lord, open my lips,
And my mouth shall show forth Your praise.
For You do not desire sacrifice, or else I would
    give it;
You do not delight in burnt offering.
The sacrifices of God are a broken spirit,
A broken and a contrite heart—
These, O God, You will not despise.

Ps. 51:14-17

O God, You know my foolishness;
And my sins are not hidden from You.
Let not those who wait for You, O Lord GOD of
    hosts, be ashamed because of me;
Let not those who seek You be confounded because
    of me, O God of Israel.   Ps. 69:5, 6

You are merciful and gracious,
Slow to anger, and abounding in mercy.
You will not always strive with us,

Nor will You keep Your anger forever.
You have not dealt with us according to our sins,
Nor punished us according to our iniquities.
For as the heavens are high above the earth,
So great is Your mercy toward those who fear You;
As far as the east is from the west,
So far have You removed our transgressions from us.
As a father pities his children,
So the LORD pities those who fear Him.
For You know our frame;
You remember that we are dust.   Ps. 103:8-14

We have sinned with our fathers,
We have committed iniquity,
We have done wickedly.   Ps. 106:6

O GOD the Lord,
Deal with me for Your name's sake;
Because Your mercy is good, deliver me.
                                           Ps. 109:21

Out of the depths I have cried to You, O LORD;
Lord, hear my voice!
Let Your ears be attentive
To the voice of my supplications.
If You, LORD, should mark iniquities,
O Lord, who could stand?
But there is forgiveness with You,
That You may be feared.   Ps. 130:1-4

Search me, O God, and know my heart;
Try me, and know my anxieties;

And see if there is any wicked way in me,
And lead me in the way everlasting.

Ps. 139:23, 24

For there is not a just man on earth who does good
And does not sin.   Eccl. 7:20

"Come now, and let us reason together,"
Says the LORD,
"Though your sins are like scarlet,
They shall be as white as snow;
Though they are red like crimson,
They shall be as wool."   Is. 1:18

Woe is me, for I am undone!
Because I am a man of unclean lips.   Is. 6:5

For thus says the Lord GOD, the Holy One of Israel:
"In returning and rest you shall be saved;
In quietness and confidence shall be your strength."

Is. 30:15

I, even I, am He who blots out your transgressions
    for My own sake;
And I will not remember your sins.   Is. 43:25

I have blotted out, like a thick cloud, your
    transgressions,
And like a cloud, your sins.
Return to Me, for I have redeemed you.   Is. 44:22

Who among you fears the LORD?
Who obeys the voice of His Servant?

Who walks in darkness
And has no light?
Let him trust in the name of the LORD
And rely upon his God.   Is. 50:10

But He was wounded for our transgressions,
He was bruised for our iniquities;
The chastisement for our peace was upon Him,
And by His stripes we are healed.
All we like sheep have gone astray;
We have turned, every one, to his own way;
And the LORD has laid on Him the iniquity of us all.
                                                Is. 53:5, 6

For a mere moment I have forsaken you,
But with great mercies I will gather you.
With a little wrath I hid My face from you for a
    moment;
But with everlasting kindness I will have mercy on
    you.   Is. 54:7, 8

May I seek You while You may be found,
May I call upon You while You are near.
Let the wicked forsake his way,
And the unrighteous man his thoughts;
Let him return to You,
And You will have compassion on him;
And to our God,
For You will abundantly pardon.   Is. 55:6, 7

For our transgressions are multiplied before You,
And our sins testify against us;
For our transgressions are with us,

And as for our iniquities, we know them:
In transgressing and lying against the LORD,
And departing from our God,
Speaking oppression and revolt,
Conceiving and uttering from the heart words of
    falsehood.   Is. 59:12, 13

But on this one will I look:
On him who is poor and of a contrite spirit,
And who trembles at My word.   Is. 66:2

O LORD, I know the way of man is not in himself;
It is not in man who walks to direct his own steps.
O LORD, correct me, but with justice;
Not in Your anger, lest You bring me to nothing.
                                            Jer. 10:23, 24

The heart is deceitful above all things,
And desperately wicked;
Who can know it?
You, the LORD, search the heart,
You test the mind,
Even to give every man according to his ways,
According to the fruit of his doings.   Jer. 17:9, 10

Heal me, O LORD, and I shall be healed;
Save me, and I shall be saved,
For You are my praise.   Jer. 17:14

I will cleanse them from all their iniquity by which
they have sinned against Me, and I will pardon all
their iniquities by which they have sinned and by
which they have transgressed against Me.

                                            Jer. 33:8

May I search out and examine my ways,
And turn back to You.   Lam. 3:40

Come, and let us return to the LORD;
For He has torn, but He will heal us;
He has stricken, but He will bind us up.
After two days He will revive us;
On the third day He will raise us up,
That we may live in His sight.   Hos. 6:1, 2

I return to the LORD my God,
For I have stumbled because of my iniquity.
I take words with me,
And return to the LORD.
I say to Him,
"Take away all iniquity;
Receive me graciously,
For I will offer the sacrifices of my lips."
                                    Hos. 14:1, 2

"Now, therefore," says the LORD,
"Turn to Me with all your heart,
With fasting, with weeping, and with mourning."
So rend your heart, and not your garments;
Return to the LORD your God,
For He is gracious and merciful,
Slow to anger, and of great kindness;
And He relents from doing harm.   Joel 2:12, 13

When my soul fainted within me,
I remembered the LORD;
And my prayer went up to You,
Into Your holy temple.

Those who regard worthless idols
Forsake their own Mercy.
But I will sacrifice to You
With the voice of thanksgiving;
I will pay what I have vowed.
Salvation is of the LORD.   Jon. 2:7-9

You will again have compassion on us,
And will subdue our iniquities.   Mic. 7:19

O LORD, I have heard Your speech and was afraid.
O LORD, revive Your work in the midst of the years!
In the midst of the years make it known;
In wrath remember mercy.   Hab. 3:2

May I bear fruits worthy of repentance.   Matt. 3:8

"Lord, how often shall my brother sin against me and
I forgive him? Up to seven times?" Jesus said to him,
"I do not say to you, up to seven times, but up to
seventy times seven."   Matt. 18:21, 22

No temptation has overtaken you except such as is
common to man; but God is faithful, who will not
allow you to be tempted beyond what you are able,
but with the temptation will also make the way of
escape, that you may be able to bear it.
                                        1 Cor. 10:13

My son, do not despise the chastening of the LORD,
Nor be discouraged when you are rebuked by Him;
For whom the LORD loves He chastens,
And scourges every son whom He receives.

Now no chastening seems to be joyful for the present, but painful; nevertheless, afterward it yields the peaceable fruit of righteousness to those who have been trained by it. Therefore strengthen the hands which hang down, and the feeble knees, and make straight paths for your feet, so that what is lame may not be dislocated, but rather be healed.

Heb. 12:5, 6, 11-13

If we say that we have no sin, we deceive ourselves, and the truth is not in us. If we confess our sins, He is faithful and just to forgive us our sins and to cleanse us from all unrighteousness.   1 John 1:8, 9

If anyone sins, we have an Advocate with the Father, Jesus Christ the righteous. And He Himself is the propitiation for our sins, and not for ours only but also for the whole world.   1 John 2:1, 2

Prayers for Renewal

May I have no other gods before You.
May I not make for myself [an idol].
May I not take Your name in vain.
May I remember the Sabbath day, to keep it holy.
May I honor my father and my mother.
May I not murder.
May I not commit adultery.
May I not steal.
May I not bear false witness against my neighbor.
May I not covet my neighbor's possessions.

Ex. 20:3-17

Now therefore, I pray, if I have found grace in Your sight, show me now Your way, that I may know You and that I may find grace in Your sight.   Ex. 33:13

May I consecrate myself, and be holy, for You are the LORD my God.   Lev. 20:7

Hear, O Israel: The LORD our God, the LORD is one! You shall love the LORD your God with all your heart, with all your soul, and with all your strength.

                                                Deut. 6:4, 5

And now, what does the LORD your God require of you, but to fear Him, to walk in all His ways and to love Him, to serve Him with all your heart and with all your soul?   Deut. 10:12

May I never pervert justice; nor show partiality, nor take a bribe, for a bribe blinds the eyes of the wise and twists the words of the righteous.

                                               Deut. 16:19

This Book of the Law shall not depart from your mouth, but you shall meditate in it day and night, that you may observe to do according to all that is written in it. For then you will make your way prosperous, and then you will have good success.

                                                 Josh. 1:8

May I fear You, and serve You in truth with all my heart; for I consider what great things You have done for me.   1 Sam. 12:24

Therefore give to Your servant an understanding heart
to judge Your people, that I may discern between
good and evil.   1 Kin. 3:9

May the LORD our God be with me, as You were with
our fathers. Do not leave me nor forsake me,
that You may incline my heart to You, to walk in all
Your ways, and to keep Your commandments and
Your statutes and Your judgments, which You
commanded our fathers. Let my heart therefore be
loyal to You, to walk in Your statutes and keep Your
commandments as at this day.   1 Kin. 8:57, 58, 61

Show me Your ways, O LORD;
Teach me Your paths.
Lead me in Your truth and teach me,
For You are the God of my salvation;
On You I wait all the day.
Remember, O LORD, Your tender mercies and Your
    lovingkindnesses,
For they are from of old.   Ps. 25:4-6

Come, you children, listen to me;
I will teach you the fear of the LORD.
Who is the man who desires life,
And loves many days, that he may see good?
Keep your tongue from evil,
And your lips from speaking deceit:
Depart from evil and do good;
Seek peace and pursue it.
The eyes of the LORD are on the righteous,
And His ears are open to their cry.   Ps. 34:11-15

Trust in the LORD, and do good;
Dwell in the land, and feed on His faithfulness.
Delight yourself also in the LORD,
And He shall give you the desires of your heart.
Commit your way to the LORD,
Trust also in Him,
And He shall bring it to pass.
He shall bring forth your righteousness as the light,
And your justice as the noonday.   Ps. 37:3-6

LORD, make me to know my end,
And what is the measure of my days,
That I may know how frail I am.   Ps. 39:4

May I defend the poor and fatherless;
Do justice to the afflicted and needy.
Deliver the poor and needy;
Free them from the hand of the wicked.
                                        Ps. 82:3, 4

So teach me to number my days,
That I may gain a heart of wisdom.   Ps. 90:12

I will set nothing wicked before my eyes;
I hate the work of those who fall away;
It shall not cling to me.   Ps. 101:3

I will meditate on Your precepts,
And contemplate Your ways.
I will delight myself in Your statutes;
I will not forget Your word.
Deal bountifully with Your servant,
That I may live and keep Your word.

Open my eyes, that I may see
Wondrous things from Your law.   Ps. 119:15-18

Incline my heart to Your testimonies,
And not to covetousness.
Turn away my eyes from looking at worthless things,
And revive me in Your way.   Ps. 119:36, 37

Direct my steps in Your word,
And let no iniquity have dominion over me.
                                        Ps. 119:133

Search me, O God, and know my heart;
Try me, and know my anxieties;
And see if there is any wicked way in me,
And lead me in the way everlasting.
                                        Ps. 139:23, 24

Set a guard, O LORD, over my mouth;
Keep watch over the door of my lips.
Do not incline my heart to any evil thing.
                                        Ps. 141:3, 4

Cause me to hear Your lovingkindness in the
      morning,
For in You do I trust;
Cause me to know the way in which I should walk,
For I lift up my soul to You.
Teach me to do Your will,
For You are my God;
Your Spirit is good.
Lead me in the land of uprightness.   Ps. 143:8, 10

May I honor You with my possessions,
And with the firstfruits of all my increase.

Prov. 3:9

May I keep my heart with all diligence,
For out of it spring the issues of life.
May I put away a deceitful mouth,
And put perverse lips far from me.
Let my eyes look straight ahead,
And my eyelids look right before me.
May I ponder the path of my feet,
And all my ways will be established.
May I not turn to the right or the left;
But remove my foot from evil.   Prov. 4:23-27

May I apply my heart to instruction,
And my ears to words of knowledge.   Prov. 23:12

These things I shall do:
Speak the truth to my neighbor;
Give judgment in your gates for truth, justice, and
   peace;
Not think evil in my heart against my neighbor;
Nor love a false oath.
For all these are things that You hate.

Zech. 8:16, 17

Blessed are the poor in spirit,
   For theirs is the kingdom of heaven.
Blessed are those who mourn,
   For they shall be comforted.
Blessed are the meek,
   For they shall inherit the earth.

51

Blessed are those who hunger and thirst for
    righteousness,
  For they shall be filled.
Blessed are the merciful,
  For they shall obtain mercy.
Blessed are the pure in heart,
  For they shall see God.
Blessed are the peacemakers,
  For they shall be called sons of God.
Blessed are those who are persecuted for
    righteousness' sake,
  For theirs is the kingdom of heaven.

Matt. 5:3-10

May my light so shine before men that they may see
my good works and glorify my Father in heaven.

Matt. 5:16

Our Father in heaven,
Hallowed be Your name.
Your kingdom come,
Your will be done
On earth as it is in heaven.
Give us this day our daily bread.
And forgive us our debts,
As we forgive our debtors.
And do not lead us into temptation,
But deliver us from the evil one.
For Yours is the kingdom and the power and the glory
    forever. Amen.   Matt. 6:9-13

May I seek first Your kingdom and Your
righteousness, and may all these things be
added to me.

Matt. 6:33

Therefore, whatever you want men to do to you, do also to them, for this is the Law and the Prophets.

Matt. 7:12

Having found one pearl of great price, may I go and sell all that I have, and buy it.   Matt. 13:46

You shall love the LORD your God with all your heart, with all your soul, and with all your mind.

Matt. 22:37

You shall love your neighbor as yourself.

Matt. 22:39

His lord said to him, "Well done, good and faithful servant; you were faithful over a few things, I will make you ruler over many things. Enter into the joy of your lord."   Matt. 25:21

May I love my enemies, do good, and lend, hoping for nothing in return; and my reward will be great, and I will be a son of the Most High. For You are kind to the unthankful and evil.   Luke 6:35

No servant can serve two masters; for either he will hate the one and love the other, or else he will be loyal to the one and despise the other. You cannot serve God and mammon.   Luke 16:13

If you abide in Me, and My words abide in you, you will ask what you desire, and it shall be done for you. By this My Father is glorified, that you bear much fruit; so you will be My disciples. As the Father loved Me, I also have loved you; abide in My love. If

you keep My commandments, you will abide in My
love, just as I have kept My Father's commandments
and abide in His love. These things I have spoken to
you, that My joy may remain in you, and that your joy
may be full.   John 15:7-11

I was buried with Christ through baptism into death,
that just as He was raised from the dead by Your
glory, even so I also should walk in newness of life.
For if I have been united with Him in the likeness of
His death, certainly I also shall be in the likeness of
His resurrection, knowing this, that my old man was
crucified with Him, that the body of sin might be
done away with, that I should no longer be a slave
of sin.   Rom. 6:4-6

May I not go on presenting the members of my body
as instruments of unrighteousness to sin, but may I
present myself to You as being alive from the dead,
and my members as instruments of righteousness to
You.   Rom. 6:13

May I, by Your mercies, present my body a living
sacrifice, holy, acceptable to You, which is my
reasonable service. And may I not be conformed to
this world, but be transformed by the renewing of
my mind, that I may prove what is Your good and
acceptable and perfect will.   Rom. 12:1, 2

May I love without hypocrisy, abhor what is evil,
cling to what is good. May I be kindly affectionate to
others with brotherly love, in honor giving preference
to others; not lagging in diligence, fervent in spirit,
serving the Lord; rejoicing in hope, patient in

tribulation, continuing steadfastly in prayer; distributing to the needs of the saints, given to hospitality.   Rom. 12:9-13

May I put on the Lord Jesus Christ, and make no provision for the flesh, to fulfill its lusts.
                                                        Rom. 13:14

It is required in stewards that one be found faithful.
                                                        1 Cor. 4:2

May I flee sexual immorality. Every sin that a man does is outside the body, but he who commits sexual immorality sins against his own body.   1 Cor. 6:18

I was bought at a price; therefore may I glorify You in my body and in my spirit, which are Yours.
                                                        1 Cor. 6:20

Whether I eat or drink, or whatever I do, may I do all to the glory of God.   1 Cor. 10:31

Love suffers long and is kind; love does not envy; love does not parade itself, is not puffed up; does not behave rudely, does not seek its own, is not provoked, thinks no evil; does not rejoice in iniquity, but rejoices in the truth; bears all things, believes all things, hopes all things, endures all things. Love never fails.   1 Cor. 13:4-8

I pray that I may be steadfast, immovable, always abounding in the work of the Lord, knowing that my labor is not in vain in the Lord.   1 Cor. 15:58

May I cast down arguments and every high thing that exalts itself against the knowledge of You, and bring every thought into captivity to the obedience of Christ.   2 Cor. 10:5

May the God of our Lord Jesus Christ, the Father of glory give me the spirit of wisdom and revelation in the knowledge of Him. I pray that the eyes of my understanding may be enlightened; that I may know what is the hope of His calling, what are the riches of the glory of His inheritance in the saints, and what is the exceeding greatness of His power toward us who believe, according to the working of His mighty power which He worked in Christ when He raised Him from the dead and seated Him at His right hand in the heavenly places, far above all principality and power and might and dominion, and every name that is named, not only in this age, but also in that which is to come.   Eph. 1:17-21

By Your grace, may I walk worthy of the calling with which I was called, with all lowliness and gentleness, with longsuffering, bearing with others in love, endeavoring to keep the unity of the Spirit in the bond of peace.   Eph. 4:1-3

May no corrupt word proceed out of my mouth, but what is good for necessary edification, that it may impart grace to the hearers. May I not grieve the Holy Spirit of God, by whom I was sealed for the day of redemption. May all bitterness, wrath, anger, clamor, and evil speaking be put away from me, with all malice. And may I be kind to others,

tenderhearted, forgiving others, even as God in
Christ forgave me.   Eph. 4:29-32

By Your grace may we not be drunk with wine, in
which is dissipation; but be filled with the Spirit,
speaking to one another in psalms and hymns and
spiritual songs, singing and making melody in our
hearts to the Lord, giving thanks always for all things
to God the Father in the name of our Lord Jesus
Christ, submitting to one another in the fear of God.
                                            Eph. 5:18-21

May I be strong in the Lord and in the power of His
might as I put on the whole armor of God, that I may
be able to stand against the wiles of the devil.
                                            Eph. 6:10, 11

May I take up the whole armor of God, that I may be
able to withstand in the evil day, and having done all,
to stand. May I stand therefore, having girded my
waist with truth, having put on the breastplate of
righteousness, and having shod my feet with the
preparation of the gospel of peace; above all, taking
the shield of faith with which I will be able to quench
all the fiery darts of the wicked one. And may I take
the helmet of salvation, and the sword of the Spirit,
which is the word of God; praying always with all
prayer and supplication in the Spirit, being watchful
to this end with all perseverance and supplication for
all the saints.   Eph. 6:13-18

May my love abound still more and more in
knowledge and all discernment, that I may approve

the things that are excellent, that I may be sincere
and without offense till the day of Christ, being filled
with the fruits of righteousness which are by Jesus
Christ, to the glory and praise of God.

Phil. 1:9-11

May I do nothing from selfish ambition or conceit,
but in lowliness of mind let me esteem others better
than myself, not merely looking out for my own
interests, but also for the interests of others.

Phil. 2:3, 4

May I do all things without complaining and disputing,
that I may become blameless and harmless, a child of
God without fault in the midst of a crooked and
perverse generation, among whom I shine as a light in
the world, holding fast the word of life.

Phil. 2:14-16

May I count all things loss for the excellence of the
knowledge of Christ Jesus my Lord, for whom I have
suffered the loss of all things, and count them as
rubbish, that I may gain Christ and be found in Him,
not having my own righteousness, which is from the
law, but that which is through faith in Christ, the
righteousness which is from You by faith; that I may
know Him and the power of His resurrection, and the
fellowship of His sufferings, being conformed to His
death.   Phil. 3:8-10

I do not count myself to have apprehended; but one
thing I do, forgetting those things which are behind
and reaching forward to those things which are

ahead, I press toward the goal for the prize of the
upward call of God in Christ Jesus.   Phil. 3:13, 14

May I be anxious for nothing, but in everything by
prayer and supplication, with thanksgiving, may my
requests be made known to You; and Your peace,
which surpasses all understanding, will guard my
heart and mind through Christ Jesus.   Phil. 4:6, 7

Whatever things are true, whatever things are noble,
whatever things are just, whatever things are pure,
whatever things are lovely, whatever things are of
good report, if there is any virtue and if there is
anything praiseworthy—may I meditate on these
things.   Phil. 4:8

May I be filled with the knowledge of Your will in all
wisdom and spiritual understanding; that I may walk
worthy of You, fully pleasing You, being fruitful in
every good work and increasing in the knowledge of
God; strengthened with all might, according to Your
glorious power, for all patience and longsuffering with
joy; giving thanks to the Father who has qualified me
to partake of the inheritance of the saints in the
light.   Col. 1:9-12

Lord, since I have been raised with Christ, may I
seek those things which are above, where Christ is,
sitting at the right hand of God. May I set my mind
on things above, not on things on the earth. For I
have died, and my life is hidden with Christ in You.
When Christ who is my life appears, then I also will
appear with Him in glory.   Col. 3:1-4

May I put to death my members which are on the
earth: fornication, uncleanness, passion, evil desire,
and covetousness, which is idolatry.   Col. 3:5

Therefore, as the elect of God, holy and beloved,
may I put on tender mercies, kindness, humility,
meekness, longsuffering; bearing with others and
forgiving others, if anyone has a complaint against
another; even as Christ forgave me, so I also must
do. But above all these things may I put on love,
which is the bond of perfection. And may the peace
of God rule in my heart, that I may be thankful. May
the word of Christ dwell in me richly in all wisdom,
teaching and admonishing others in psalms and
hymns and spiritual songs, singing with grace in my
heart to the Lord. And whatever I do in word or
deed, may I do all in the name of the Lord Jesus,
giving thanks to God the Father through Him.
                                                    Col. 3:12-17

Grant that I may walk in wisdom toward those who
are outside, redeeming the time. May my speech
always be with grace, seasoned with salt, that I
may know how I ought to answer each one.
                                                    Col. 4:5, 6

May I rejoice always, pray without ceasing, in
everything give thanks; for this is the will of God in
Christ Jesus for me. May I not quench the Spirit or
despise prophecies, but test all things; hold fast to
what is good, and abstain from every form of evil.
                                                    1 Thess. 5:16-22

May I be diligent to present myself approved to You,
as a worker who does not need to be ashamed,
rightly dividing the word of truth.   2 Tim. 2:15

Seeing then that I have a great High Priest who has
passed through the heavens, Jesus the Son of God,
may I hold fast my confession. For I do not have
a High Priest who cannot sympathize with my
weaknesses, but was in all points tempted as I am,
yet without sin. I therefore come boldly to the throne
of grace, that I may obtain mercy and find grace to
help in time of need.   Heb. 4:14-16

May I lay aside every weight, and the sin which so
easily ensnares me, and may I run with endurance the
race that is set before me, looking unto Jesus, the
author and finisher of my faith, who for the joy that
was set before Him endured the cross, despising the
shame, and has sat down at the right hand of the
throne of God.   Heb. 12:1, 2

Let my conduct be without covetousness; being
content with what I have. For You Yourself have
said, "I will never leave you nor forsake you."
                                       Heb. 13:5

May I count it all joy when I fall into various trials,
knowing that the testing of my faith produces
patience. And let patience have its perfect work,
that I may be perfect and complete, lacking nothing.
Grant that if I lack wisdom, I may ask of You, who
give to all liberally and without reproach, and it will
be given to me.   James 1:2-5

May I submit to You and resist the devil that he may
flee from me. James 4:7

May my faith, being much more precious than gold
that perishes, though it is tested by fire, be found
to praise, honor, and glory at the revelation of Jesus
Christ. 1 Pet. 1:7

Grant that I may gird the loins of my mind, be sober,
and rest my hope fully upon the grace that is to be
brought to me at the revelation of Jesus Christ; as an
obedient child, may I not be conformed to the former
lusts, as in my ignorance; but as He who called me is
holy, may I also be holy in all my conduct, because it
is written, "Be holy, for I am holy." 1 Pet. 1:13-16

Father, as a sojourner and pilgrim, grant that I may
abstain from fleshly lusts which wage war against
my soul. 1 Pet. 2:11

May I be of one mind with others, compassionate,
loving as a brother, tenderhearted, courteous, not
returning evil for evil or reviling for reviling, but on
the contrary blessing, knowing that I was called to
this, that I may inherit a blessing. 1 Pet. 3:8, 9

May I sanctify Christ as Lord in my heart, and
always be ready to give a defense to everyone who
asks me a reason for the hope that is in me, with
meekness and fear. 1 Pet. 3:15

Grant that I may clothe myself with humility toward
others, for

"You resist the proud,
But give grace to the humble."

Therefore, may I humble myself under Your mighty
hand that You may exalt me in due time, casting all
my care upon You, because You care for me.

1 Pet. 5:5-7

By Your grace may I be sober and vigilant; because
my adversary the devil walks about like a roaring
lion, seeking whom he may devour. May I resist
him, steadfast in the faith, knowing that the same
sufferings are experienced by my brotherhood in the
world.

1 Pet. 5:8, 9

Giving all diligence, may I add to my faith virtue,
to virtue knowledge, to knowledge self-control, to
self-control perseverance, to perseverance godliness,
to godliness brotherly kindness, and to brotherly
kindness love.

2 Pet. 1:5-7

Prayers for Personal Needs

Please, show me Your glory.

Ex. 33:18

Rise up, O LORD!
Let Your enemies be scattered,
And let those who hate You flee before You.

Num. 10:35

Yet regard the prayer of Your servant and his
supplication, O LORD my God, and listen to the cry

and the prayer which Your servant is praying before
You today.   1 Kin. 8:28

Oh, that You would bless me indeed, and enlarge my
territory, that Your hand would be with me, and that
You would keep me from evil, that I may not cause
pain!   1 Chr. 4:10

LORD, it is nothing for You to help, whether with
many or with those who have no power; help us, O
LORD our God, for we rest on You, and in Your name
we go against this multitude. O LORD, You are our
God; do not let man prevail against You!"
                                            2 Chr. 14:11

O Lord, I pray, please let Your ear be attentive to the
prayer of Your servant, and to the prayer of Your
servants who desire to fear Your name; and let Your
servant prosper this day, I pray, and grant him mercy
in the sight of this man.   Neh. 1:11

Remember me, O my God, for good!   Neh. 13:31

Oh, that I might have my request,
That You would grant me the thing that I long for!
                                              Job 6:8

Hear me when I call,
O God of my righteousness!
You have relieved me in my distress;
Have mercy on me, and hear my prayer.   Ps. 4:1

Give ear to my words, O LORD,
Consider my meditation.

Give heed to the voice of my cry,
My King and my God,
For to You I will pray.
My voice You shall hear in the morning, O LORD;
In the morning I will direct it to You,
And I will look up.   Ps. 5:1-3

But as for me, I will come into Your house in the
    multitude of Your mercy;
In fear of You I will worship toward Your holy temple.
Lead me, O LORD, in Your righteousness because of
    my enemies;
Make Your way straight before my face.
                                        Ps. 5:7, 8

O LORD my God, in You I put my trust;
Save me from all those who persecute me;
And deliver me.   Ps. 7:1

But You, O LORD, do not be far from Me;
O My Strength, hasten to help Me!   Ps. 22:19

Turn Yourself to me, and have mercy on me,
For I am desolate and afflicted.
The troubles of my heart have enlarged;
Bring me out of my distresses!
Look on my affliction and my pain,
And forgive all my sins.   Ps. 25:16-18

My times are in Your hand;
Deliver me from the hand of my enemies,
And from those who persecute me.
Make Your face shine upon Your servant;
Save me for Your mercies' sake.   Ps. 31:15, 16

May I let not the foot of pride come against me,
Nor the hand of the wicked drive me away.

Ps. 36:11

Do not withhold Your tender mercies from me, O
    LORD;
Let Your lovingkindness and Your truth continually
    preserve me.   Ps. 40:11

Be merciful to me, O God, be merciful to me!
For my soul trusts in You;
And in the shadow of Your wings I will make my
    refuge,
Until these calamities have passed by.
I will cry out to God Most High,
To God who performs all things for me.

Ps. 57:1, 2

God be merciful to us and bless us,
And cause His face to shine upon us,
That Your way may be known on earth,
Your salvation among all nations.   Ps. 67:1, 2

O God, do not be far from me;
O my God, make haste to help me!   Ps. 71:12

Give ear, O LORD, to my prayer;
And attend to the voice of my supplications.
In the day of my trouble I will call upon You,
For You will answer me.   Ps. 86:6, 7

With my whole heart I have sought You;
Oh, let me not wander from Your commandments!
Your word I have hidden in my heart,

That I might not sin against You.
Blessed are You, O Lord!
Teach me Your statutes.   Ps. 119:10-12

Make me understand the way of Your precepts;
So shall I meditate on Your wondrous works.
My soul melts from heaviness;
Strengthen me according to Your word.

                                           Ps. 119:27, 28

Deal with Your servant according to Your mercy,
And teach me Your statutes.   Ps. 119:124

Out of the depths I have cried to You, O Lord;
Lord, hear my voice!
Let Your ears be attentive
To the voice of my supplications.   Ps. 130:1, 2

Lord, I cry out to You;
Make haste to me!
Give ear to my voice when I cry out to You.
Let my prayer be set before You as incense,
The lifting up of my hands as the evening sacrifice.
Set a guard, O Lord, over my mouth;
Keep watch over the door of my lips.
Do not incline my heart to any evil thing,
To practice wicked works
With men who work iniquity;
And do not let me eat of their delicacies.

                                           Ps. 141:1-4

Hear my prayer, O Lord,
Give ear to my supplications!

In Your faithfulness answer me,
And in Your righteousness.　　　　　　Ps. 143:1

Cause me to hear Your lovingkindness in the
　　morning,
For in You do I trust;
Cause me to know the way in which I should walk,
For I lift up my soul to You.　　　　　Ps. 143:8

Teach me to do Your will,
For You are my God;
Your spirit is good.
Lead me in the land of uprightness.　　Ps. 143:10

I called on Your name, O LORD,
From the lowest pit.
You have heard my voice:
"Do not hide Your ear
From my sighing, from my cry for help."
You drew near on the day I called on You,
And said, "Do not fear!"
O Lord, You have pleaded the case for my soul;
You have redeemed my life.　　　　Lam. 3:55-58

Ask, and it will be given to you; seek, and you will
find; knock, and it will be opened to you. For
everyone who asks receives, and he who seeks finds,
and to him who knocks it will be opened.
　　　　　　　　　　　　　　　　　Matt. 7:7, 8

Now may the God of patience and comfort grant you
to be like-minded toward one another, according to
Christ Jesus, that you may with one mind and one

mouth glorify the God and Father of our Lord Jesus
Christ.   Rom. 15:5, 6

Seeing then that we have a great High Priest who
has passed through the heavens, Jesus the Son of
God, let us hold fast our confession. For we do not
have a High Priest who cannot sympathize with our
weaknesses, but was in all points tempted as we are,
yet without sin. Let us therefore come boldly to the
throne of grace, that we may obtain mercy and find
grace to help in time of need.   Heb. 4:14-16

Little children, keep yourselves from idols. Amen.
                                              1 John 5:21

"Surely I am coming quickly." Amen. Even so, come,
Lord Jesus!   Rev. 22:20

Prayers for Others

And these words, which I command you today shall
be in your heart. You shall teach them diligently to
your children, and shall talk of them when you sit in
your house, when you walk by the way, when you lie
down, when you rise up.   Deut. 6:6, 7

Moreover, as for me, far be it from me that I should
sin against the LORD in ceasing to pray for you; but
I will teach you the good and the right way.
                                              1 Sam. 12:23

Incline Your ear, O LORD, and hear; open Your eyes,
O LORD, and see.   2 Kin. 19:16

O LORD God of Abraham, Isaac, and Israel, our
fathers, keep this forever in the intent of the
thoughts of the heart of Your people, and fix
their heart toward You.   1 Chr. 29:18

So we fasted and entreated You for this, and You
answered our prayer.   Ezra 8:23

Salvation belongs to the LORD.
Your blessing is upon Your people.   Ps. 3:8

There are many who say,
"Who will show us any good?"
LORD, lift up the light of Your countenance upon us.
                                            Ps. 4:6

But let all those rejoice who put their trust in You;
Let them ever shout for joy, because You defend
    them;
Let those also who love Your name
Be joyful in You.   Ps. 5:11

Restore us, O God of our salvation,
And cause Your anger toward us to cease.
Will You be angry with us forever?
Will You prolong Your anger to all generations?
Will You not revive us again,
That Your people may rejoice in You?
Show us Your mercy, LORD,
And grant us Your salvation.   Ps. 85:4-7

The LORD will perfect that which concerns me;
Your mercy, O LORD, endures forever;

May I not forsake the works of Your hands.

Ps. 138:8

Why do You forget us forever,
And forsake us for so long a time?
Turn us back to You, O LORD, and we will be
    restored;
Renew our days as of old.

Lam. 5:20, 21

May I set my face toward You to make request by
prayer and supplications, with fasting, sackcloth, and
ashes. May I pray to You, and make confession, and
say, "O Lord, great and awesome God, who keeps
Your covenant and mercy with those who love You,
and with those who keep Your commandments, we
have sinned and committed iniquity, we have done
wickedly and rebelled, even by departing from Your
precepts and Your judgments. To You belong mercy
and forgiveness, though we have rebelled against You.
We have not obeyed Your voice, to walk in Your laws,
which You set before us by Your servants the
prophets.

Dan. 9:3-5, 9, 10

Our Father in heaven,
Hallowed be Your name.
Your kingdom come.
Your will be done
On earth as it is in heaven.

Matt. 6:9, 10

The harvest truly is plentiful, but the laborers are
few. Therefore pray the Lord of the harvest to send
out laborers into His harvest.

Matt. 9:37, 38

Again I say to you that if two of you agree on earth concerning anything that they ask, it will be done for them by My Father in heaven. For where two or three are gathered together in My name, I am there in the midst of them. Matt. 18:19, 20

Now in the morning, having risen a long while before daylight, He went out and departed to a solitary place; and there He prayed. Mark 1:35

I do not pray for these alone, but also for those who will believe in Me through their word; that they all may be one, as You, Father, are in Me, and I in You; that they also may be one in Us, that the world may believe that You sent Me. John 17:20, 21

God is my witness, whom I serve with my spirit in the gospel of His Son, that without ceasing I make mention of you always in my prayers. Rom. 1:9

Likewise the Spirit also helps in our weaknesses. For we do not know what we should pray for as we ought, but the Spirit Himself makes intercession for us with groanings which cannot be uttered. Now He who searches the hearts knows what the mind of the Spirit is because He makes intercession for the saints according to the will of God. Rom. 8:26, 27

Bear one another's burdens, and so fulfill the law of Christ. Gal. 6:2

Therefore I also, after I heard of your faith in the Lord Jesus and your love for all the saints, do not

cease to give thanks for you, making mention of you
in my prayers. Eph. 1:15, 16

May the God of our Lord Jesus Christ, the Father
of glory, give to you the spirit of wisdom and
revelation in the knowledge of Him, the eyes of your
understanding being enlightened; that you may know
what is the hope of His calling, what are the riches
of the glory of His inheritance in the saints, and what
is the exceeding greatness of His power toward us
who believe, according to the working of His mighty
power which He worked in Christ when He raised
Him from the dead and seated Him at His right hand
in the heavenly places, far above all principality and
power and might and dominion, and every name that
is named, not only in this age but also in that which
is to come. Eph. 1:17-21

For this reason I bow my knees to the Father of our
Lord Jesus Christ, from whom the whole family in
heaven and earth is named, that He would grant
you, according to the riches of His glory, to be
strengthened with might through His Spirit in the
inner man, that Christ may dwell in your hearts
through faith; that you, being rooted and grounded
in love, may be able to comprehend with all the
saints what is the width and length and depth and
height—to know the love of Christ which passes
knowledge; that you may be filled with all the
fullness of God. Eph. 3:14-19

May I pray always with all prayer and supplication
in the Spirit, being watchful to this end with all

perseverance and supplication for all the saints. And for me, that utterance may be given to me, that I may open my mouth boldly to make known the mystery of the gospel.   Eph. 6:18, 19

This I pray, that your love may abound still more and more in knowledge and all discernment, that you may approve the things that are excellent, that you may be sincere and without offense till the day of Christ, being filled with the fruits of righteousness which are by Jesus Christ, to the glory and praise of God.
                                                   Phil. 1:9, 11

May I be anxious for nothing, but in everything by prayer and supplication, with thanksgiving, let my requests be made known to You.   Phil. 4:6

For this reason we also, since the day we heard it, do not cease to pray for you, and to ask that you may be filled with the knowledge of His will in all wisdom and spiritual understanding; that you may have a walk worthy of the Lord, fully pleasing Him, being fruitful in every good work and increasing in the knowledge of God; strengthened with all might, according to His glorious power, for all patience and longsuffering with joy; giving thanks to the Father who has qualified us to be partakers of the inheritance of the saints in the light.
                                                   Col. 1:9-12

Continue earnestly in prayer, being vigilant in it with thanksgiving; meanwhile praying also for us, that God would open to us a door for the word, to speak the mystery of Christ.   Col. 4:2, 3

Now may our God and Father Himself, and our Lord
Jesus Christ, direct our way to you. And may the
Lord make you increase and abound in love to one
another and to all, just as we do to you.

1 Thess. 3:11, 12

Brethren, pray for us. 1 Thess. 5:25

Therefore we also pray always for you that our God
would count you worthy of this calling, and fulfill all
the good pleasure of His goodness and the work of
faith with power, that the name of our Lord Jesus
Christ may be glorified in you, and you in Him,
according to the grace of our God and the Lord
Jesus Christ. 2 Thess. 1:11, 12

But we are bound to give thanks to God always for
you, brethren beloved by the Lord, because God
from the beginning chose you for salvation through
sanctification by the Spirit and belief in the truth, to
which He called you by our gospel, for the obtaining
of the glory of our Lord Jesus Christ.

2 Thess. 2:13, 14

Now may our Lord Jesus Christ Himself, and our
God and Father, who has loved us and given us
everlasting consolation and good hope by grace,
comfort your hearts and establish you in every good
word and work. 2 Thess. 2:16, 17

Finally, brethren, pray for us, that the word of the
Lord may run swiftly and be glorified, just as it
is with you, and that we may be delivered from
unreasonable and wicked men; for not all have faith.

2 Thess. 3:1, 2

Now may the Lord direct your hearts into the love of God and into the patience of Christ.   2 Thess. 3:5

Therefore I exhort first of all that supplications, prayers, intercessions, and giving of thanks be made for all men, for kings and all who are in authority, that we may lead a quiet and peaceable life in all godliness and reverence. For this is good and acceptable in the sight of God our Savior, who desires all men to be saved and to come to the knowledge of the truth.   1 Tim. 2:1-4

I thank my God, making mention of you always in my prayers, hearing of your love and faith which you have toward the Lord Jesus and toward all the saints.
Philem. 4, 5

Confess your trespasses to one another, and pray for one another, that you may be healed. The effective, fervent prayer of a righteous man avails much.
James 5:16

The end of all things is at hand; therefore be serious and watchful in your prayers.   1 Pet. 4:7

I pray that you may prosper in all things and be in health, just as your soul prospers.   3 John 2

Prayers of Affirmation

For You are my lamp, O LORD;
The LORD shall enlighten my darkness.

For by You I can run against a troop;
By my God I can leap over a wall.

2 Sam. 22:29, 30

But who am I, and who are my people,
That we should be able to offer so willingly as this?
For all things come from You,
And of Your own we have given You.   1 Chr. 29:14

Your eyes run to and fro throughout the whole earth,
to show Yourself strong on behalf of those whose
heart is loyal to You.   2 Chr. 16:9

I prepare my heart to seek the Law of the LORD, and
to do it, and to teach Your statutes and ordinances.

Ezra 7:10

Your hand is upon all those for good who seek You,
but Your power and Your wrath are against all those
who forsake You.   Ezra 8:22

For You, O LORD, will bless the righteous;
With favor You will surround him as with a shield.

Ps. 5:12

O LORD, You are the portion of my inheritance and
    my cup;
You maintain my lot.
The lines have fallen to me in pleasant places;
Yes, I have a good inheritance.   Ps. 16:5, 6

You are my light and my salvation;
Whom shall I fear?

You are the strength of my life;
Of whom shall I be afraid?   Ps. 27:1

Instruct me and teach me in the way I should go;
You will guide me with Your eye.   Ps. 32:8

And now, Lord, what do I wait for?
My hope is in You.   Ps. 39:7

Blessed is that man who makes the LORD his trust,
And does not respect the proud, nor such as turn
    aside to lies.   Ps. 40:4

I delight to do Your will, O my God,
And Your law is within my heart.   Ps. 40:8

If I cast my burden on the LORD,
He shall sustain me;
He shall never permit the righteous to be moved.
                                              Ps. 55:22

Before I was afflicted I went astray,
But now I keep Your word.
It is good for me that I have been afflicted,
That I may learn Your statutes.
I know, O LORD, that Your judgments are right,
And that in faithfulness You have afflicted me.
                                    Ps. 119:67, 71, 75

Your word is a lamp to my feet
And a light to my path.   Ps. 119:105

Unless the LORD builds the house,
We labor in vain who build it;

Unless the LORD guards the city,
The watchman stays awake in vain.   Ps. 127:1

Yes, if you cry out for discernment,
And lift up your voice for understanding,
If you seek her as silver,
And search for her as for hidden treasures;
Then you will understand the fear of the LORD,
And find the knowledge of God.
For the LORD gives wisdom;
From His mouth come knowledge and understanding;
He stores up sound wisdom for the upright;
He is a shield to those who walk uprightly.
                                           Prov. 2:3-7

The fear of the LORD is the beginning of wisdom,
And the knowledge of the Holy One is understanding.
                                           Prov. 9:10

For unto us a Child is born,
Unto us a Son is given;
And the government will be upon His shoulder.
And His name will be called
Wonderful, Counselor, Mighty God,
Everlasting Father, Prince of Peace.   Is. 9:6, 7

Behold, God is my salvation,
I will trust and not be afraid;
For YAH, the LORD, is my strength and song;
He also has become my salvation.   Is. 12:2

You will keep him in perfect peace,
Whose mind is stayed on You,
Because he trusts in You.   Is. 26:3

Have you not known?
Have you not heard?
The everlasting God, the LORD,
The Creator of the ends of the earth,
Neither faints nor is weary.
His understanding is unsearchable.
He gives power to the weak,
And to those who have no might He increases
    strength.
Even the youths shall faint and be weary,
And the young men shall utterly fall,
But those who wait on the LORD
Shall renew their strength;
They shall mount up with wings like eagles,
They shall run and not be weary,
They shall walk and not faint.   Is. 40:28-31

I will fear not, for You are with me;
I will not be dismayed, for You are my God.
You will strengthen me,
You will help me,
You will uphold me with Your righteous right hand.
                                Is. 41:10

"For My thoughts are not your thoughts,
Nor are your ways My ways," says the LORD.
"For as the heavens are higher than the earth,
So are My ways higher than your ways,
And My thoughts than your thoughts."   Is. 55:8, 9

Let not the wise man glory in his wisdom,
Let not the mighty man glory in his might,
Nor let the rich man glory in his riches;

But let him who glories glory in this,
That he understands and knows You,
That You are the LORD, exercising lovingkindness,
    judgment, and righteousness in the earth.
For in these You delight.   Jer. 9:23, 24

You are good to those who wait for You,
To the soul who seeks You.
It is good that we should hope and wait quietly
For the salvation of the LORD.   Lam. 3:25, 26

You have shown us what is good;
And what do You require of us
But to do justly,
To love mercy,
And to walk humbly with You?   Mic. 6:8

"Not by might nor by power, but by My Spirit,"
Says the LORD of hosts.   Zech. 4:6

I shall not lay up for myself treasures on earth,
where moth and rust destroy and where thieves break
in and steal; but I shall lay up for myself treasures in
heaven, where neither moth nor rust destroys and
where thieves do not break in and steal.
                         Matt. 6:19, 20

I may come to You, weary and heavy laden, and You
will give me rest. I may take Your yoke upon me, and
learn from You, for You are gentle and lowly in heart,
and I shall find rest for my soul. For Your yoke is
easy, and Your burden is light.   Matt. 11:28-30

You so loved the world that You gave Your only
begotten Son, that whoever believes in Him should
not perish but have everlasting life. You did not send
Your Son into the world to condemn the world, but
that the world through Him might be saved.

John 3:16, 17

Whoever drinks of the water that You shall give him
will never thirst. But the water that You shall give
him will become in him a fountain of water springing
up into eternal life.   John 4:14

You are Spirit, and we who worship You must
worship in spirit and truth.   John 4:24

He who hears Your word and believes in Him who
sent You has everlasting life, and shall not come into
judgment, but has passed from death into life.

John 5:24

You are the bread of life. He who comes to You shall
never hunger, and he who believes in You shall never
thirst.   John 6:35

All that the Father gives You will come to You, and
the one who comes to You You will by no means cast
out.   John 6:37

You are the living bread which came down from
heaven. If anyone eats of this bread, he will live
forever; and the bread that You gave is Your
flesh, which You gave for the life of the world.

John 6:51

You are the light of the world. He who follows You shall not walk in the darkness, but have the light of life. John 8:12

I shall know the truth, and the truth shall make me free. John 8:32

You are the door. If anyone enters by You he will be saved, and will go in and out and find pasture. The thief does not come except to steal, and to kill, and to destroy. You have come that we may have life, and that we may have it more abundantly. You are the good shepherd. The good shepherd gives His life for the sheep. John 10:9-11

Your sheep hear Your voice, and You know them, and they follow You. And You give them eternal life, and they shall never perish; neither shall anyone snatch them out of Your hand. The Father, who has given them to You, is greater than all; and no one is able to snatch them out of the Father's hand. You and the Father are one. John 10:27-30

You are the resurrection and the life. He who believes in You, though he may die, he shall live. And whoever lives and believes in You shall never die.
John 11:25, 26

You are the way, the truth, and the life. No one comes to the Father except through You.
John 14:6

Whatever we ask in Your name, that You will do, that the Father may be glorified in the Son. John 14:13

If we love You, we will keep Your commandments.

John 14:15

He who has Your commandments and keeps them, it is he who loves You. And he who loves You will be loved by Your Father, and You will love him and manifest Yourself to him.

John 14:21

If anyone loves You, he will keep Your word; and Your Father will love him, and You will come to him and make Your home with him.

John 14:23

If we keep Your commandments, we will abide in Your love, just as You have kept Your Father's commandments and abide in His love.

John 15:10

This is Your commandment, that we love one another as You have loved us.

John 15:12

No longer do You call us servants, for a servant does not know what his master is doing; but You have called us friends, for all things that You heard from Your Father You have made known to us.

John 15:15

We did not choose You, but You chose us and appointed us that we should go and bear fruit, and that our fruit should remain, that whatever we ask the Father in Your name He may give us.

John 15:16

These things You have spoken to us, that in You we may have peace. In the world we will have tribulation; but we are of good cheer, You have overcome the world.   John 16:33

This is eternal life, that we may know You, the only true God, and Jesus Christ whom You have sent.
                                                    John 17:3

If we believe on the Lord Jesus Christ, we will be saved, we and our household.   Acts 16:31

I am not ashamed of the gospel of Christ, for it is Your power to salvation for everyone who believes, for the Jew first and also for the Greek. For in it Your righteousness is revealed from faith to faith; as it is written, "The just shall live by faith."
                                                    Rom. 1:16, 17

We all have sinned and fall short of Your glory, being justified freely by Your grace through the redemption that is in Christ Jesus.   Rom. 3:23, 24

Having been justified by faith, I have peace with God through my Lord Jesus Christ, through whom also I have access by faith into this grace in which I stand, and rejoice in hope of the glory of God.
                                                    Rom. 5:1, 2

You demonstrated Your own love toward us, in that while we were still sinners, Christ died for us.
                                                    Rom. 5:8

I reckon myself to be dead indeed to sin, but alive to God in Christ Jesus our Lord.   Rom. 6:11

The wages of sin is death, but Your gift is eternal life in Christ Jesus our Lord.   Rom. 6:23

There is therefore now no condemnation to us who are in Christ Jesus, who do not walk according to the flesh, but according to the Spirit. For the law of the Spirit of life in Christ Jesus has made us free from the law of sin and death.   Rom. 8:1, 2

For I have not received the spirit of bondage again to fear, but I have received the Spirit of adoption by whom I cry out, "Abba, Father."   Rom. 8:15

Your Spirit Himself bears witness with our spirit that we are Your children, and if children, then heirs—Your heirs and joint heirs with Christ, if indeed we suffer with Him, that we may also be glorified together.   Rom. 8:16, 17

For I consider that the sufferings of this present time are not worthy to be compared with the glory which shall be revealed in me.   Rom. 8:18

The Spirit also helps in our weaknesses. For we do not know what we should pray for as we ought, but the Spirit Himself makes intercession for us with groanings which cannot be uttered.   Rom. 8:26

We know that all things work together for good to those who love You, to those who are the called according to Your purpose. For whom You foreknew, You also predestined to be conformed to the image of Your Son, that He might be the firstborn among many brethren. Moreover whom You predestined, these You also called; whom You called, these You also justified; and whom You justified, these You also glorified. Rom. 8:28-30

You who did not spare Your own Son, but delivered Him up for us all, how shall You not with Him also freely give us all things? Rom. 8:32

I am persuaded that neither death nor life, nor angels nor principalities nor powers, nor things present nor things to come, nor height nor depth, nor any other created thing, shall be able to separate me from the love of God which is in Christ Jesus my Lord.
Rom. 8:38, 39

If we confess with our mouth the Lord Jesus and believe in our heart that You have raised Him from the dead, we will be saved. For with the heart one believes to righteousness, and with the mouth confession is made to salvation. For the Scripture says, "Whoever believes on Him will not be put to shame." Rom. 10:9-11

Eye has not seen, nor ear heard,
Nor have entered into the heart of man
The things which You have prepared for those who
love You. 1 Cor. 2:9

My body is the temple of the Holy Spirit who is in me, whom I have from God, and I am not my own. For I have been bought with a price; therefore I will glorify God in my body and in my spirit, which are God's. 1 Cor. 6:19

No temptation has overtaken us except such as is common to man; but God is faithful, who will not allow us to be tempted beyond what we are able, but with the temptation will also make the way of escape, that we may be able to bear it.

1 Cor. 10:13

Love suffers long and is kind; love does not envy; love does not parade itself, is not puffed up; does not behave rudely, does not seek its own, is not provoked, thinks no evil; does not rejoice in iniquity, but rejoices in the truth; bears all things, believes all things, hopes all things, endures all things.

1 Cor. 13:4-7

Blessed are You, the God and Father of our Lord Jesus Christ, the Father of mercies and God of all comfort, who comforts us in all our tribulation, that we may be able to comfort those who are in any trouble, with the comfort with which we ourselves are comforted by You.

2 Cor. 1:3, 4

For it is the God who commanded light to shine out of darkness, who has shone in our hearts to give the light of the knowledge of the glory of God in the face of Jesus Christ. But we have this treasure in earthen vessels, that the excellence of the power may be of God and not of us.

2 Cor. 4:6, 7

Therefore I do not lose heart. Even though my outward man is perishing, yet my inward man is being renewed day by day. For our light affliction, which is but for a moment, is working for me a far more exceeding and eternal weight of glory, while I look not at the things which are seen, but at the things which are not seen. For the things which are seen are temporary, but the things which are not seen are eternal. 2 Cor. 4:16-18

I am always confident, knowing that while I am at home in the body I am absent from the Lord. For I walk by faith, not by sight. I am confident, yes, well pleased rather to be absent from the body and to be present with the Lord. 2 Cor. 5:6-8

I have it as my aim, whether present or absent, to be well pleasing to Him. For we must all appear before the judgment seat of Christ, that each one may receive the things done in the body, according to what he has done, whether good or bad.
2 Cor. 5:9, 10

Since I am in Christ, I am a new creation; old things have passed away; behold, all things have become new. 2 Cor. 5:17

You made Him who knew no sin to be sin for us, that we might become Your righteousness in Him.
2 Cor. 5:21

We know Your grace, that though You were rich, yet for our sakes You became poor, that we through Your poverty might become rich. 2 Cor. 8:9

But this I say: He who sows sparingly will also reap sparingly, and he who sows bountifully will also reap bountifully. So let each one give as he purposes in his

heart, not grudgingly or of necessity; for God loves a
cheerful giver. 2 Cor. 9:6, 7

For the weapons of our warfare are not carnal but
mighty in God for pulling down strongholds, casting
down arguments and every high thing that exalts
itself against the knowledge of God, bringing every
thought into captivity to the obedience of Christ.
2 Cor. 10:4, 5

And He said to me, "My grace is sufficient for you,
for My strength is made perfect in weakness."
Therefore most gladly, I will rather boast in my
infirmities, that the power of Christ may rest upon
me. 2 Cor. 12:9

I have been crucified with Christ; it is no longer I
who live, but Christ lives in me; and the life which I
now live in the flesh I live by faith in the Son of God,
who loved me and gave Himself for me. Gal. 2:20

By grace I have been saved through faith, and that
not of myself; it is the gift of God, not of works, lest
anyone should boast. For I am His workmanship,
created in Christ Jesus for good works, which God
prepared beforehand that I should walk in them.
Eph. 2:8, 9

For to me, to live is Christ, and to die is gain.
Phil. 1:21

You delivered me from the power of darkness and
conveyed me into the kingdom of the Son of Your

love, in whom I have redemption through His blood, the forgiveness of sins. Col. 1:13, 14

You are the image of the invisible God, the firstborn over all creation. For by You all things were created that are in heaven and that are on earth, visible and invisible, whether thrones or dominions or principalities or powers. All things were created through You and for You. You are before all things, and in You all things consist. And You are the head of the body, the church, who is the beginning, the firstborn from the dead, that in all things You may have the preeminence. Col. 1:15-18

There is one God and one Mediator between God and men, the Man Christ Jesus, who gave Himself a ransom for all, to be testified in due time.
1 Tim. 2:5, 6

You were manifested in the flesh,
Justified in the Spirit,
Seen by angels,
Preached among the Gentiles,
Believed on in the world,
Received up in glory. 1 Tim. 3:16

For You have not given us a spirit of fear, but of power and of love and of a sound mind.
2 Tim. 1:7

I know whom I have believed and am persuaded that He is able to keep what I have committed to Him until that Day. 2 Tim. 1:12

All Scripture is given by inspiration of God, and is profitable for doctrine, for reproof, for correction, for instruction in righteousness, that the man of God may be complete, thoroughly equipped for every good work. 2 Tim. 3:16, 17

When Your kindness and love toward man appeared, not by works of righteousness which we have done, but according to Your mercy You saved us, through the washing of regeneration and renewing of the Holy Spirit, whom You poured out on us abundantly through Jesus Christ our Savior, that having been justified by His grace we should become heirs according to the hope of eternal life. Titus 3:4-7

The word of God is living and powerful, and sharper than any two-edged sword, piercing even to the division of soul and spirit, and of joints and marrow, and is a discerner of the thoughts and intents of the heart. And there is no creature hidden from His sight, but all things are naked and open to the eyes of Him to whom we must give account.
Heb. 4:12, 13

As it is appointed for men to die once, but after this the judgment, so You were offered once to bear the sins of many. To those who eagerly wait for You You will appear a second time, apart from sin for salvation. Heb. 9:27, 28

Now faith is the substance of things hoped for, the evidence of things not seen. Heb. 11:1

But without faith it is impossible to please Him, for
he who comes to God must believe that He is, and
that He is a rewarder of those who diligently seek
Him.   Heb. 11:6

Jesus Christ is the same yesterday, today, and
forever.   Heb. 13:8

Every good gift and every perfect gift is from above,
and comes down from You, the Father of lights, with
whom there is no variation or shadow of turning.
                                                  James 1:17

All that is in the world—the lust of the flesh, the lust
of the eyes, and the pride of life—is not of the Father
but is of the world. And the world is passing away,
and the lust of it; but he who does the will of God
abides forever.   1 John 2:16, 17

Behold what manner of love the Father has bestowed
on us, that we should be called children of God!
Therefore the world does not know us, because it did
not know Him. Beloved, now we are children of God;
and it has not yet been revealed what we shall be,
but we know that when He is revealed, we shall be
like Him, for we shall see Him as He is.
                                               1 John 3:1, 2

We know that we have passed from death to life,
because we love the brethren. He who does not love
his brother abides in death.
                                               1 John 3:14

By this we know love, because You laid down Your
life for us. And we also ought to lay down our lives
for the brethren.   1 John 3:16

This is Your commandment: that we should believe
on the name of Your Son Jesus Christ and love one
another, as You gave us commandment.
                                                     1 John 3:23

There is no fear in love; but perfect love casts out
fear, because fear involves torment. But he who fears
has not been made perfect in love.   1 John 4:18

He who overcomes shall be clothed in white
garments, and You will not blot out his name from
the Book of Life; but You will confess his name
before Your Father and before His angels.   Rev. 3:5

You stand at the door and knock. If anyone hears
Your voice and opens the door, You will come in to
him and dine with him, and he with You.   Rev. 3:20

To him who overcomes You will grant to sit with You
on Your throne, as You also overcame and sat down
with Your Father on His throne.   Rev. 3:21

You are worthy to take the scroll,
And to open its seals,
For You were slain,
And have redeemed us to God by Your blood
Out of every tribe and tongue and people and nation.
                                                     Rev. 5:9

Behold, You are coming quickly, and Your reward is with You, to give to every one according to his work. You are the Alpha and the Omega, the Beginning and the End, the First and the Last.   Rev. 22:12, 13

Prayers of Thanksgiving

You in Your mercy have led forth
The people whom You have redeemed;
You have guided them in Your strength
To Your holy habitation.   Ex. 15:13

O Lord GOD, You have begun to show Your servant Your greatness and Your mighty hand, for what god is there in heaven or on earth who can do anything like Your works and Your mighty deeds?   Deut. 3:24

My heart rejoices in the LORD;
My horn is exalted in the LORD,
I smile at my enemies,
Because I rejoice in Your salvation.
No one is holy like the LORD,
For there is none besides You,
Nor is there any rock like our God.   1 Sam. 2:1, 2

You are my rock and my fortress and my deliverer;
The God of my strength, in whom I will trust;
My shield and the horn of my salvation,
My stronghold and my refuge;
My Savior, You save me from violence.
                                        2 Sam. 22:2, 3

I will call upon the LORD, who is worthy to be
    praised;
So shall I be saved from my enemies.   2 Sam. 22:4

For who is God, except the LORD?
And who is a rock, except our God?
God is my strength and power,
And He makes my way perfect.
He makes my feet like the feet of deer,
And sets me on my high places.   2 Sam. 22:32-34

Oh, give thanks to the LORD!
Call upon His name;
Make known His deeds among the peoples!
Sing to Him, sing psalms to Him;
Talk of all His wondrous works!
Glory in His holy name;
Let the hearts of those rejoice who seek the LORD!
Seek the LORD and His strength;
Seek His face evermore!
Remember His marvelous works which He has done,
His wonders, and the judgments of His mouth.
    1 Chr. 16:8-12

Sing to the LORD, all the earth;
Proclaim the good news of His salvation from day to
    day.
Declare His glory among the nations,
His wonders among all peoples.
For the LORD is great and greatly to be praised;
He is also to be feared above all gods.
For all the gods of the peoples are idols,
But the LORD made the heavens.

Honor and majesty are before Him,
Strength and gladness are in His place.

1 Chr. 16:23-27

Oh, give thanks to the LORD, for He is good!
For His mercy endures forever.

1 Chr. 16:34

I will both lie down in peace, and sleep;
For You alone, O LORD, make me dwell in safety.

Ps. 4:8

I will praise the LORD according to His
    righteousness,
And will sing praise to the name of the LORD Most
    High.   Ps. 7:17

I will praise You, O LORD, with all my heart;
I will tell of all Your marvelous works.
I will be glad and rejoice in You;
I will sing praise to Your name, O Most High.

Ps. 9:1, 2

I have trusted in Your mercy;
My heart shall rejoice in Your salvation.
I will sing to the LORD,
Because He has dealt bountifully with me.

Ps. 13:5, 6

The LORD is my light and my salvation;
Whom shall I fear?
The LORD is the strength of my life;
Of whom shall I be afraid?   Ps. 27:1

Blessed be the LORD,
Because He has heard the voice of my supplications!
The LORD is my strength and my shield;
My heart trusted in Him, and I am helped;
Therefore my heart greatly rejoices,
And with my song I will praise Him.

Ps. 28:6, 7

I will extol You, O LORD, for You have lifted me up,
And have not let my foes rejoice over me.
O LORD my God, I cried out to You,
And You healed me.

Ps. 30:1, 2

Oh, how great is Your goodness,
Which You have laid up for those who fear You,
Which You have prepared for those who trust in You
In the presence of the sons of men!

Ps. 31:19

Oh, love the LORD, all you His saints!
For the LORD preserves the faithful,
And fully repays the proud person.
Be of good courage,
And He shall strengthen your heart,
All you who hope in the LORD.

Ps. 31:23, 24

Our soul waits for the LORD;
He is our help and our shield.
For our heart shall rejoice in Him,
Because we have trusted in His holy name.
Let Your mercy, O LORD, be upon us,
Just as we hope in You.

Ps. 33:20-22

I waited patiently for You;
And You inclined to me,

And heard my cry.
You also brought me up out of a horrible pit,
Out of the miry clay,
And set my feet upon a rock,
And established my steps.
You have put a new song in my mouth—
Praise to You;
Many will see it and fear,
And will trust in You.   Ps. 40:1-3

Many, O LORD my God, are Your wonderful works
Which You have done;
And Your thoughts toward us
Cannot be recounted to You in order;
If I would declare and speak of them,
They are more than can be numbered.   Ps. 40:5

Why are you cast down, O my soul?
And why are you disquieted within me?
Hope in God;
For I shall yet praise Him,
The help of my countenance and my God.

                                          Ps. 42:11

God is our refuge and strength,
A very present help in trouble.   Ps. 46:1

But I will sing of Your power;
Yes, I will sing aloud of Your mercy in the morning;
For You have been my defense
And refuge in the day of my trouble.
To You, O my Strength, I will sing praises;
For God is my defense,
My God of mercy.   Ps. 59:16, 17

Truly my soul silently waits for God;
From Him comes my salvation.
He alone is my rock and my salvation;
He is my defense;
I shall not be greatly moved.   Ps. 62:1, 2

The righteous shall be glad in the LORD, and trust in
    Him.
And all the upright in heart shall glory.   Ps. 64:10

Whom have I in heaven but You?
And there is none upon earth that I desire besides
    You.
My flesh and my heart fail;
But God is the strength of my heart and my portion
    forever.   Ps. 73:25, 26

We give thanks to You, O God, we give thanks!
For Your wondrous works declare that Your name is
    near.   Ps. 75:1

Mercy and truth have met together;
Righteousness and peace have kissed.
Truth shall spring out of the earth,
And righteousness shall look down from heaven.
                                    Ps. 85:10, 11

I will sing of the mercies of the LORD forever;
With my mouth will I make known Your faithfulness
    to all generations.
For I have said, "Mercy shall be built up forever;
Your faithfulness You shall establish in the very
    heavens."   Ps. 89:1, 2

He who dwells in the secret place of the Most High
Shall abide under the shadow of the Almighty.
I will say of the LORD, "He is my refuge and my
    fortress;
My God, in Him I will trust."   Ps. 91:1, 2

Because he has set his love upon Me, therefore I will
    deliver him;
I will set him on high, because he has known My
    name.
He shall call upon Me, and I will answer him;
I will be with him in trouble;
I will deliver him and honor him.
With long life I will satisfy him,
And show him My salvation.   Ps. 91:14-16

Bless the LORD, O my soul;
And all that is within me, bless His holy name!
Bless the LORD, O my soul,
And forget not all His benefits:
Who forgives all your iniquities,
Who heals all your diseases,
Who redeems your life from destruction,
Who crowns you with lovingkindness and tender
    mercies,
Who satisfies your mouth with good things,
So that your youth is renewed like the eagle's.
                        Ps. 103:1-5

Oh, give thanks to the LORD!
Call upon His name;
Make known His deeds among the peoples!
Sing to Him, sing psalms to Him;

Talk of all His wondrous works!
Glory in His holy name;
Let the hearts of those rejoice who seek the LORD!
Seek the LORD and His strength;
Seek His face evermore!
Remember His marvelous works which He has done,
His wonders, and the judgments of His mouth.

Ps. 105:1-5

Praise the LORD!
Oh, give thanks to the LORD, for He is good!
For His mercy endures forever.
Who can utter the mighty acts of the LORD?
Who can declare all His praise?   Ps. 106:1, 2

The works of the LORD are great,
Studied by all who have pleasure in them.
His work is honorable and glorious,
And His righteousness endures forever.
He has made His wonderful works to be
    remembered;
The LORD is gracious and full of compassion.

Ps. 111:2-4

Oh, give thanks to the God of heaven!
For His mercy endures forever.   Ps. 136:26

All the kings of the earth shall praise You, O LORD,
When they hear the words of Your mouth.
Yes, they shall sing of the ways of the LORD,
For great is the glory of the LORD.
Though the LORD is on high,
Yet He regards the lowly;
But the proud He knows from afar.   Ps. 138:4-6

O LORD, You are my God.
I will exalt You,
I will praise Your name,
For You have done wonderful things;
Your counsels of old are faithfulness and truth.

Is. 25:1

I will greatly rejoice in the LORD,
My soul shall be joyful in my God;
For He has clothed me with the garments of
    salvation,
He has covered me with the robe of righteousness,
As a bridegroom decks himself with ornaments,
And as a bride adorns herself with her jewels.

Is. 61:10

Through the LORD's mercies we are not consumed,
Because His compassions fail not.
They are new every morning;
Great is Your faithfulness.   Lam. 3:22, 23

I will look to the LORD;
I will wait for the God of my salvation;
My God will hear me.   Mic. 7:7

But to you who fear My name
The Sun of Righteousness shall arise
With healing in His wings;
And you shall go out
And grow fat like stall-fed calves.   Mal. 4:2

Thanks be to God, who gives us the victory through
our Lord Jesus Christ.   1 Cor. 15:57

Now thanks be to God who always leads us in triumph in Christ, and through us diffuses the fragrance of His knowledge in every place.

2 Cor. 2:14

Rejoice in the Lord always. Again I will say, rejoice!

Phil. 4:4

Therefore by Him let us continually offer the sacrifice of praise to God, that is, the fruit of our lips, giving thanks to His name.

Heb. 13:15

Blessed be the God and Father of our Lord Jesus Christ, who according to His abundant mercy has begotten us again to a living hope through the resurrection of Jesus Christ from the dead, to an inheritance incorruptible and undefiled and that does not fade away, reserved in heaven for you, who are kept by the power of God through faith for salvation ready to be revealed in the last time.

1 Pet. 1:3-5

We give You thanks, O Lord God Almighty,
The One who is and who was and who is to come,
Because You have taken Your great power and
  reigned.

Rev. 11:17

Closing Prayers

The LORD bless you and keep you;
The LORD make His face shine upon you,
And be gracious to you;

The LORD lift up His countenance upon you,
And give you peace.   Num. 6:24-26

I will both lie down in peace, and sleep;
For You alone, O LORD, make me dwell in safety.
                                        Ps. 4:8

You will show me the path of life;
In Your presence is fullness of joy;
At Your right hand are pleasures forevermore.
                                        Ps.16:11

Let the words of my mouth and the meditation
     of my heart
Be acceptable in Your sight,
O LORD, my strength and my Redeemer.
                                        Ps. 19:14

Surely goodness and mercy shall follow me
All the days of my life;
And I will dwell in the house of the LORD
Forever.   Ps. 23:6

I would have lost heart, unless I had believed
That I would see the goodness of the LORD
In the land of the living.
Wait on the LORD;
Be of good courage,
And He shall strengthen your heart;
Wait, I say, on the LORD!   Ps. 27:13, 14

Save Your people,
And bless Your inheritance;

Shepherd us also,
And bear us up forever. Ps. 28:9

Be of good courage,
And He shall strengthen your heart,
All you who hope in the LORD. Ps. 31:24

Be glad in the LORD and rejoice, you righteous;
And shout for joy, all you upright in heart!
Ps. 32:11

The LORD will command His lovingkindness in the
    daytime,
And in the night His song shall be with me —
A prayer to the God of my life. Ps. 42:8

But it is good for me to draw near to God;
I have put my trust in the Lord GOD,
That I may declare all Your works. Ps. 73:28

I will remember the works of the LORD;
Surely I will remember Your wonders of old.
I will also meditate on all Your work,
And talk of Your deeds. Ps. 77:11, 12

For a day in Your courts is better than a thousand.
I would rather be a doorkeeper in the house of my
    God
Than dwell in the tents of wickedness.
For the LORD God is a sun and shield;
The LORD will give grace and glory;
No good thing will He withhold
From those who walk uprightly.

O LORD of hosts,
Blessed is the man who trusts in You!

Ps. 84:10-12

Blessed be the LORD forevermore!
Amen and Amen.   Ps. 89:52

So teach us to number our days,
That we may gain a heart of wisdom.   Ps. 90:12

Oh, satisfy us early with Your mercy,
That we may rejoice and be glad all our days!

Ps. 90:14

And let the beauty of the LORD our God be upon us,
And establish the work of our hands for us;
Yes, establish the work of our hands.   Ps. 90:17

Bless the LORD, all you His hosts,
You ministers of His, who do His pleasure.
Bless the LORD, all His works,
In all places of His dominion.
Bless the LORD, O my soul!   Ps. 103:21, 22

This is the day the LORD has made;
We will rejoice and be glad in it.   Ps. 118:24

The LORD shall preserve you from all evil;
He shall preserve your soul.
The LORD shall preserve your going out and your
      coming in
From this time forth, and even forevermore.

Ps. 121:7, 8

Great is our Lord, and mighty in power;
His understanding is infinite.
The LORD lifts up the humble;
He casts the wicked down to the ground.

Ps. 147:5, 6

Glory to God in the highest,
And on earth peace, goodwill toward men!

Luke 2:14

Now may the God of patience and comfort grant us
to be like-minded toward one another, according to
Christ Jesus, that we may with one mind and one
mouth glorify the God and Father of our Lord Jesus
Christ.

Rom. 15:5, 6

Now may the God of hope fill us with all joy and
peace in believing, that we may abound in hope by
the power of the Holy Spirit.

Rom. 15:13

Now to Him who is able to establish us according to
the gospel and the preaching of Jesus Christ, to God,
alone wise, be glory through Jesus Christ forever.
Amen.

Rom. 16:25, 27

Blessed be the God and Father of our Lord Jesus
Christ, the Father of mercies and God of all comfort,
who comforts us in all our tribulation, that we may
be able to comfort those who are in any trouble, with
the comfort with which we ourselves are comforted
by God.

2 Cor. 1:3, 4

Finally, brethren, farewell. Become complete. Be of
good comfort, be of one mind, live in peace; and the

God of love and peace will be with you. The grace of
the Lord Jesus Christ, and the love of God, and the
communion of the Holy Spirit, be with us all.

2 Cor. 13:11, 14

Now to Him who is able to do exceedingly
abundantly above all that we ask or think,
according to the power that works in us, to
Him be glory in the church by Christ Jesus to all
generations, forever and ever. Amen.   Eph. 3:20, 21

Now may the God of peace sanctify us completely;
and may our whole spirit, soul, and body be
preserved blameless at the coming of our Lord
Jesus Christ.   1 Thess. 5:23

Now may our Lord Jesus Christ Himself, and our
God and Father, who has loved us and given us
everlasting consolation and good hope by grace,
comfort our hearts and establish us in every good
word and work.   2 Thess. 2:16, 17

Now to the King eternal, immortal, invisible, to God
who alone is wise, be honor and glory forever and
ever. Amen.   1 Tim. 1:17

He who is the blessed and only Potentate, the
King of kings and Lord of lords, who alone has
immortality, dwelling in unapproachable light, whom
no man has seen or can see, to whom be
honor and everlasting power. Amen.   1 Tim. 6:15, 16

Grace, mercy, and peace from God the Father and the
Lord Jesus Christ our Savior.   Titus 1:4

Now may the God of peace who brought up our Lord
Jesus from the dead, that great Shepherd of the
sheep, through the blood of the everlasting covenant,
make us complete in every good work to do His will,
working in us what is well pleasing in His sight,
through Jesus Christ, to whom be glory forever and
ever. Amen.   Heb. 13:20, 21

May the God of all grace, who called us to His
eternal glory by Christ Jesus, after we have suffered
a while, perfect, establish, strengthen, and settle us.
To Him be the glory and the dominion forever and
ever. Amen.   1 Pet. 5:10, 11

Grow in the grace and knowledge of our Lord and
Savior Jesus Christ. To Him be the glory both now
and forever. Amen.   2 Pet. 3:18

Now to Him who is able to keep us from stumbling,
And to present us faultless
Before the presence of His glory with exceeding joy,
To God our Savior,
Who alone is wise,
Be glory and majesty,
Dominion and power,
Both now and forever.
Amen.   Jude 24, 25

Blessing and honor and glory and power
Be to Him who sits on the throne,
And to the Lamb, forever and forever!   Rev. 5:13

Blessing and glory and wisdom,
Thanksgiving and honor and power and might,
Be to our God forever and ever.   Rev. 7:12

Part II
Guides to Bible Reading and Bible Memorization

How to Use the Bible Reading Guide

Purpose

The purpose of the Bible Reading Guide is to provide you with a variety of methods that will encourage and guide your reading of Scripture. Using these approaches, you can develop a personalized and manageable program that will keep your interest level high and give you a satisfying breadth of exposure to the Word of God.

How to Use It

Choose one or more of the following ten methods of Bible reading. Be flexible and feel free to change methods and combinations of methods as you desire. You may choose to integrate one method or combination with your daily prayer time and to use another method or combination at another time of the day.

Suggestions

1. Be sure to choose a system that works for you. If you find yourself getting into a rut, change your system. Many people get bored with reading the Bible because they get locked into one method.
2. Consider making a personal commitment to reading at least a chapter of the Bible a day.
3. Often the best times for Bible reading are the first thing in the morning and/or just before going to sleep.
4. If you do not have another preference, we suggest you begin your Bible reading with the 365 key chapters of the Bible (method 1 in this guide).

Bible Reading Guide

Ten Approaches to Reading the Scriptures

1. 365 key biblical chapters in a year.
2. Bible in a year, Old Testament and New Testament daily readings.
3. Bible in a year, cover to cover, on a consecutive schedule, using a six-day week for flexibility.
4. New Testament in a year, using a six-day week for flexibility.
5. Two or three chapters of the Old Testament per day (skip Psalms and/or Proverbs if also using methods 7, 8, or 9).
6. One chapter of the Gospels/Acts and one chapter of the epistles per day.
7. Five psalms (intervals of 30) and one chapter of Proverbs per day. (For example, on the first day of the month, read Psalms 1, 31, 61, 91, and 121, and Proverbs 1. On the twentieth day of the month, read Psalms 20, 50, 80, 110, and 140, and Proverbs 20.)
8. 31 key psalms per month.
9. 31 chapters of Proverbs per month according to the day of the month.
10. Psalm 119 in 22-day cycles (each day is an eight-verse stanza).

Here are some suggested combinations. Start on the level on which you can succeed.

a. Basic: methods 4 and 9.
b. Intermediate: methods 1, 8, and 9; or methods 2 and 8.
c. Advanced: methods 5, 6, and 7.

Bible Reading Guides
For
Methods 1, 2, 3, 4, and 8

METHOD 1

(365 Key Biblical Chapters in a Year)

DATE	REFERENCE	DATE	REFERENCE	DATE	REFERENCE
	JANUARY	4	Exodus 10	11	Judges 14
1	Genesis 1	5	Exodus 11	12	Judges 15
2	Genesis 3	6	Exodus 12	13	Judges 16
3	Genesis 4	7	Exodus 13	14	Ruth 1
4	Genesis 6	8	Exodus 14	15	Ruth 2
5	Genesis 7	9	Exodus 19	16	Ruth 3
6	Genesis 8	10	Exodus 20	17	Ruth 4
7	Genesis 9	11	Exodus 32	18	1 Samuel 1
8	Genesis 11	12	Leviticus 16	19	1 Samuel 2
9	Genesis 12	13	Numbers 13	20	1 Samuel 3
10	Genesis 15	14	Numbers 14	21	1 Samuel 8
11	Genesis 18	15	Deuteronomy 1	22	1 Samuel 9
12	Genesis 21	16	Deuteronomy 2	23	1 Samuel 10
13	Genesis 22	17	Deuteronomy 3	24	1 Samuel 15
14	Genesis 24	18	Deuteronomy 4	25	1 Samuel 16
15	Genesis 27	19	Deuteronomy 5	26	1 Samuel 17
16	Genesis 28	20	Deuteronomy 6	27	2 Samuel 5
17	Genesis 37	21	Deuteronomy 7	28	2 Samuel 7
18	Genesis 39	22	Deuteronomy 8	29	2 Samuel 11
19	Genesis 40	23	Deuteronomy 27	30	2 Samuel 12
20	Genesis 41	24	Deuteronomy 28	31	1 Kings 1
21	Genesis 42	25	Deuteronomy 29		**APRIL**
22	Genesis 43	26	Deuteronomy 30	1	1 Kings 2
23	Genesis 44	27	Deuteronomy 32	2	1 Kings 3
24	Genesis 45	28	Deuteronomy 34	3	1 Kings 8
25	Genesis 50		**MARCH**	4	1 Kings 9
26	Exodus 1	1	Joshua 1	5	1 Kings 10
27	Exodus 2	2	Joshua 2	6	1 Kings 11
28	Exodus 3	3	Joshua 3	7	1 Kings 12
29	Exodus 4	4	Joshua 4	8	1 Kings 17
30	Exodus 5	5	Joshua 6	9	1 Kings 18
31	Exodus 6	6	Joshua 23	10	1 Kings 19
	FEBRUARY	7	Joshua 24	11	2 Kings 1
1	Exodus 7	8	Judges 2	12	2 Kings 2
2	Exodus 8	9	Judges 6	13	2 Kings 4
3	Exodus 9	10	Judges 7	14	2 Kings 5

METHOD 1 *(continued)*

DATE	REFERENCE	DATE	REFERENCE	DATE	REFERENCE
15	2 Kings 6	22	Job 41	28	Ezekiel 37
16	2 Kings 7	23	Job 42	29	Daniel 1
17	2 Kings 8	24	Psalm 1	30	Daniel 2
18	2 Kings 18	25	Psalm 19	**JULY**	
19	2 Kings 19	26	Psalm 23	1	Daniel 3
20	2 Kings 20	27	Psalm 37	2	Daniel 4
21	2 Kings 25	28	Psalm 90	3	Daniel 5
22	1 Chronicles 17	29	Psalm 100	4	Daniel 6
23	1 Chronicles 29	30	Psalm 103	5	Daniel 9
24	1 Chronicles 34	31	Psalm 104	6	Hosea 4
25	1 Chronicles 35	**JUNE**		7	Hosea 14
26	Ezra 1	1	Psalm 105	8	Joel 2
27	Ezra 3	2	Psalm 106	9	Amos 1
28	Ezra 4	3	Psalm 107	10	Amos 2
29	Ezra 5	4	Psalm 145	11	Amos 9
30	Ezra 6	5	Proverbs 1	12	Obadiah
MAY		6	Proverbs 2	13	Jonah 1
1	Nehemiah 1	7	Proverbs 3	14	Jonah 2
2	Nehemiah 2	8	Proverbs 4	15	Jonah 3
3	Nehemiah 4	9	Proverbs 5	16	Jonah 4
4	Nehemiah 5	10	Proverbs 6	17	Micah 5
5	Nehemiah 6	11	Proverbs 7	18	Micah 7
6	Nehemiah 8	12	Proverbs 8	19	Nahum 1
7	Nehemiah 9	13	Proverbs 9	20	Habakkuk 3
8	Esther 1	14	Proverbs 31	21	Zephaniah 3
9	Esther 2	15	Ecclesiastes 3	22	Haggai 1
10	Esther 3	16	Ecclesiastes 12	23	Haggai 2
11	Esther 4	17	Song of Solomon 1	24	Zechariah 14
12	Esther 5	18	Isaiah 6	25	Malachi 3
13	Esther 6	19	Isaiah 40	26	Malachi 4
14	Esther 7	20	Isaiah 53	27	Matthew 5
15	Esther 8	21	Isaiah 55	28	Matthew 6
16	Esther 9	22	Isaiah 61	29	Matthew 7
17	Job 1	23	Jeremiah 18	30	Matthew 13
18	Job 2	24	Jeremiah 19	31	Matthew 17
19	Job 38	25	Jeremiah 31	**AUGUST**	
20	Job 39	26	Lamentations 3	1	Matthew 21
21	Job 40	27	Ezekiel 1	2	Matthew 24

METHOD 1 (continued)

DATE	REFERENCE	DATE	REFERENCE	DATE	REFERENCE
3	Matthew 25	9	Acts 16	16	2 Corinthians 12
4	Matthew 26	10	Acts 17	17	Galatians 5
5	Matthew 27	11	Acts 18	18	Galatians 6
6	Matthew 28	12	Acts 21	19	Ephesians 1
7	Mark 6	13	Acts 22	20	Ephesians 2
8	Mark 8	14	Acts 23	21	Ephesians 3
9	Luke 1	15	Acts 24	22	Ephesians 4
10	Luke 2	16	Acts 25	23	Ephesians 5
11	Luke 4	17	Acts 26	24	Ephesians 6
12	Luke 7	18	Acts 27	25	Philippians 1
13	Luke 15	19	Acts 28	26	Philippians 2
14	Luke 16	20	Romans 1	27	Philippians 3
15	Luke 18	21	Romans 2	28	Philippians 4
16	Luke 19	22	Romans 3	29	Colossians 1
17	Luke 20	23	Romans 4	30	Colossians 2
18	Luke 24	24	Romans 5	31	Colossians 3
19	John 1	25	Romans 6	**NOVEMBER**	
20	John 3	26	Romans 7	1	Colossians 4
21	John 4	27	Romans 8	2	1 Thessalonians 1
22	John 6	28	Romans 12	3	1 Thessalonians 2
23	John 8	29	Romans 13	4	1 Thessalonians 3
24	John 10	30	Romans 14	5	1 Thessalonians 4
25	John 13	**OCTOBER**		6	1 Thessalonians 5
26	John 14	1	Romans 15	7	2 Thessalonians 1
27	John 15	2	1 Corinthians 1	8	2 Thessalonians 2
28	John 16	3	1 Corinthians 2	9	2 Thessalonians 3
29	John 17	4	1 Corinthians 3	10	1 Timothy 1
30	John 20	5	1 Corinthians 6	11	1 Timothy 2
31	John 21	6	1 Corinthians 7	12	1 Timothy 3
SEPTEMBER		7	1 Corinthians 8	13	1 Timothy 4
1	Acts 1	8	1 Corinthians 9	14	1 Timothy 5
2	Acts 2	9	1 Corinthians 13	15	1 Timothy 6
3	Acts 7	10	1 Corinthians 15	16	2 Timothy 1
4	Acts 8	11	2 Corinthians 1	17	2 Timothy 2
5	Acts 9	12	2 Corinthians 4	18	2 Timothy 3
6	Acts 10	13	2 Corinthians 5	19	2 Timothy 4
7	Acts 13	14	2 Corinthians 8	20	Titus 1
8	Acts 15	15	2 Corinthians 9	21	Titus 2

METHOD 1 *(continued)*

DATE	REFERENCE	DATE	REFERENCE	DATE	REFERENCE
22	Titus 3	5	James 4	19	1 John 5
23	Philemon	6	James 5	20	2 John
24	Hebrews 1	7	1 Peter 1	21	3 John
25	Hebrews 2	8	1 Peter 2	22	Jude
26	Hebrews 4	9	1 Peter 3	23	Revelation 1
27	Hebrews 8	10	1 Peter 4	24	Revelation 2
28	Hebrews 9	11	1 Peter 5	25	Revelation 3
29	Hebrews 11	12	2 Peter 1	26	Revelation 4
30	Hebrews 12	13	2 Peter 2	27	Revelation 5
DECEMBER		14	2 Peter 3	28	Revelation 19
1	Hebrews 13	15	1 John 1	29	Revelation 20
2	James 1	16	1 John 2	30	Revelation 21
3	James 2	17	1 John 3	31	Revelation 22
4	James 3	18	1 John 4		

METHOD 2

(Bible in a Year, Old Testament and New Testament Daily Readings)

JANUARY			FEBRUARY		
Date	MORNING	EVENING	Date	MORNING	EVENING
	MATT.	GEN.		MATT.	EX.
1	1	1, 2, 3	1	21: 1-22	27, 28
2	2	4, 5, 6	2	21:23-46	29, 30
3	3	7, 8, 9	3	22: 1-22	31, 32, 33
4	4	10, 11, 12	4	22:23-46	34, 35
5	5: 1-26	13, 14, 15	5	23: 1-22	36, 37, 38
6	5:27-48	16, 17	6	23:23-39	39, 40
7	6: 1-18	18, 19			LEV.
8	6:19-34	20, 21, 22	7	24: 1-28	1, 2, 3
9	7	23, 24	8	24:29-51	4, 5
10	8: 1-17	25, 26	9	25: 1-30	6, 7
11	8:18-34	27, 28	10	25:31-46	8, 9, 10
12	9: 1-17	29, 30	11	26: 1-25	11, 12
13	9:18-38	31, 32	12	26:26-50	13
14	10: 1-20	33, 34, 35	13	26:51-75	14
15	10:21-42	36, 37, 38	14	27: 1-26	15, 16
16	11	39, 40	15	27:27-50	17, 18
17	12: 1-23	41, 42	16	27:51-66	19, 20
18	12:24-50	43, 44, 45	17	28	21, 22
19	13: 1-30	46, 47, 48		MARK	
20	13:31-58	49, 50	18	1: 1-22	23, 24
		EX.	19	1:23-45	25
21	14: 1-21	1, 2, 3	20	2	26, 27
22	14:22-36	4, 5, 6			NUM.
23	15: 1-20	7, 8	21	3: 1-19	1, 2
24	15:21-39	9, 10, 11	22	3:20-35	3, 4
25	16	12, 13	23	4: 1-20	5, 6
26	17	14, 15	24	4:21-41	7, 8
27	18: 1-20	16, 17, 18	25	5: 1-20	9, 10, 11
28	18:21-35	19, 20	26	5:21-43	12, 13, 14
29	19	21, 22	27	6: 1-29	15, 16
30	20: 1-16	23, 24	28	6:30-56	17, 18, 19
31	20:17-34	25, 26	29	7: 1-13	20, 21, 22

METHOD 2 *(continued)*

	MARCH			APRIL	
Date	MORNING	EVENING	Date	MORNING	EVENING
	MARK	**NUM.**		**LUKE**	**JUDG.**
1	7:14-37	23, 24, 25	1	6:27-49	13, 14, 15
2	8: 1-21	26, 27	2	7: 1-30	16, 17, 18
3	8:22-38	28, 29, 30	3	7:31-50	19, 20, 21
4	9: 1-29	31, 32, 33			**RUTH**
5	9:30-50	34, 35, 36	4	8: 1-25	1, 2, 3, 4
		DEUT.			**1 SAM.**
6	10: 1-31	1, 2	5	8:26-56	1, 2, 3
7	10:32-52	3, 4	6	9: 1-17	4, 5, 6
8	11: 1-18	5, 6, 7	7	9:18-36	7, 8, 9
9	11:19-33	8, 9, 10	8	9:37-62	10, 11, 12
10	12: 1-27	11, 12, 13	9	10: 1-24	13, 14
11	12:28-44	14, 15, 16	10	10:25-42	15, 16
12	13: 1-20	17, 18, 19	11	11: 1-28	17, 18
13	13:21-37	20, 21, 22	12	11:29-54	19, 20, 21
14	14: 1-26	23, 24, 25	13	12: 1-31	22, 23, 24
15	14:27-53	26, 27	14	12:32-59	25, 26
16	14:54-72	28, 29	15	13: 1-22	27, 28, 29
17	15: 1-25	30, 31	16	13:23-35	30, 31
18	15:26-47	32, 33, 34			**2 SAM.**
		JOSH.	17	14: 1-24	1, 2
19	16	1, 2, 3	18	14:25-35	3, 4, 5
	LUKE		19	15: 1-10	6, 7, 8
20	1: 1-20	4, 5, 6	20	15:11-32	9, 10, 11
21	1:21-38	7, 8, 9	21	16	12, 13
22	1:39-56	10, 11, 12	22	17: 1-19	14, 15
23	1:57-80	13, 14, 15	23	17:20-37	16, 17, 18
24	2: 1-24	16, 17, 18	24	18: 1-23	19, 20
25	2:25-52	19, 20, 21	25	18:24-43	21, 22
26	3	22, 23, 24	26	19: 1-27	23, 24
		JUDG.			**1 KIN.**
27	4: 1-30	1, 2, 3	27	19:28-48	1, 2
28	4:31-44	4, 5, 6	28	20: 1-26	3, 4, 5
29	5: 1-16	7, 8	29	20:27-47	6, 7
30	5:17-39	9, 10	30	21: 1-19	8, 9
31	6: 1-26	11, 12			

METHOD 2 *(continued)*

	MAY			JUNE	
Date	MORNING	EVENING	Date	MORNING	EVENING
	LUKE	**1 KIN.**		**JOHN**	**2 CHR.**
1	21:20-38	10, 11	1	12:27-50	15, 16
2	22: 1-20	12, 13	2	13: 1-20	17, 18
3	22:21-46	14, 15	3	13:21-38	19, 20
4	22:47-71	16, 17, 18	4	14	21, 22
5	23: 1-25	19, 20	5	15	23, 24
6	23:26-56	21, 22	6	16	25, 26, 27
		2 KIN.	7	17	28, 29
7	24: 1-35	1, 2, 3	8	18: 1-18	30, 31
8	24:36-53	4, 5, 6	9	18:19-40	32, 33
	JOHN		10	19: 1-22	34, 35, 36
9	1: 1-28	7, 8, 9			**EZRA**
10	1:29-51	10, 11, 12	11	19:23-42	1, 2
11	2	13, 14	12	20	3, 4, 5
12	3: 1-18	15, 16	13	21	6, 7, 8
13	3:19-38	17, 18		**ACTS**	
14	4: 1-30	19, 20, 21	14	1	9, 10
15	4:31-54	22, 23			**NEH.**
16	5: 1-24	24, 25	15	2: 1-21	1, 2, 3
		1 CHR.	16	2:22-47	4, 5, 6
17	5:25-47	1, 2, 3	17	3	7, 8, 9
18	6: 1-21	4, 5, 6	18	4: 1-22	10, 11
19	6:22-44	7, 8, 9	19	4:23-37	12, 13
20	6:45-71	10, 11, 12			**ESTH.**
21	7: 1-27	13, 14, 15	20	5: 1-21	1, 2
22	7:28-53	16, 17, 18	21	5:22-42	3, 4, 5
23	8: 1-27	19, 20, 21	22	6	6, 7, 8
24	8:28-59	22, 23, 24	23	7: 1-21	9, 10
25	9: 1-23	25, 26, 27			**JOB**
26	9:24-41	28, 29	24	7:22-43	1, 2
		2 CHR.	25	7:44-60	3, 4
27	10: 1-23	1, 2, 3	26	8: 1-25	5, 6, 7
28	10:24-42	4, 5, 6	27	8:26-40	8, 9, 10
29	11: 1-29	7, 8, 9	28	9: 1-21	11, 12, 13
30	11:30-57	10, 11, 12	29	9:22-43	14, 15, 16
31	12: 1-26	13, 14	30	10: 1-23	17, 18, 19

METHOD 2 *(continued)*

	JULY			AUGUST	
Date	MORNING	EVENING	Date	MORNING	EVENING
	ACTS	**JOB**		**ROM.**	**PS.**
1	10:24-48	20, 21	1	4	57, 58, 59
2	11	22, 23, 24	2	5	60, 61, 62
3	12	25, 26, 27	3	6	63, 64, 65
4	13: 1-25	28, 29	4	7	66, 67
5	13:26-52	30, 31	5	8: 1-21	68, 69
6	14	32, 33	6	8:22-39	70, 71
7	15: 1-21	34, 35	7	9: 1-15	72, 73
8	15:22-41	36, 37	8	9:16-33	74, 75, 76
9	16: 1-21	38, 39, 40	9	10	77, 78
10	16:22-40	41, 42	10	11: 1-18	79, 80
		PS.	11	11:19-36	81, 82, 83
11	17: 1-15	1, 2, 3	12	12	84, 85, 86
12	17:16-34	4, 5, 6	13	13	87, 88
13	18	7, 8, 9	14	14	89, 90
14	19: 1-20	10, 11, 12	15	15: 1-13	91, 92, 93
15	19:21-41	13, 14, 15	16	15:14-33	94, 95, 96
16	20: 1-16	16, 17	17	16	97, 98, 99
17	20:17-38	18, 19		**1 COR.**	
18	21: 1-17	20, 21, 22	18	1	100, 101, 102
19	21:18-40	23, 24, 25	19	2	103, 104
20	22	26, 27, 28	20	3	105, 106
21	23: 1-15	29, 30	21	4	107, 108, 109
22	23:16-35	31, 32	22	5	110, 111, 112
23	24	33, 34	23	6	113, 114, 115
24	25	35, 36	24	7: 1-19	116, 117, 118
25	26	37, 38, 39	25	7:20-40	119: 1-88
26	27: 1-26	40, 41, 42	26	8	119: 89-176
27	27:27-44	43, 44, 45	27	9	120, 121, 122
28	28	46, 47, 48	28	10: 1-18	123, 124, 125
	ROM.		29	10:19-33	126, 127, 128
29	1	49, 50	30	11: 1-16	129, 130, 131
30	2	51, 52, 53	31	11:17-34	132, 133, 134
31	3	54, 55, 56			

METHOD 2 *(continued)*

	SEPTEMBER			OCTOBER	
Date	MORNING	EVENING	Date	MORNING	EVENING
	1 COR.	**PS.**		**EPH.**	**IS.**
1	12	135, 136	1	4	11, 12, 13
2	13	137, 138, 139	2	5: 1-16	14, 15, 16
3	14: 1-20	140, 141, 142	3	5:17-33	17, 18, 19
4	14:21-40	143, 144, 145	4	6	20, 21, 22
5	15: 1-28	146, 147		**PHIL.**	
6	15:29-58	148, 149, 150	5	1	23, 24, 25
		PROV.	6	2	26, 27
7	16	1, 2	7	3	28, 29
	2 COR.		8	4	30, 31
8	1	3, 4, 5		**COL.**	
9	2	6, 7	9	1	32, 33
10	3	8, 9	10	2	34, 35, 36
11	4	10, 11, 12	11	3	37, 38
12	5	13, 14, 15	12	4	39, 40
13	6	16, 17, 18		**1 THESS.**	
14	7	19, 20, 21	13	1	41, 42
15	8	22, 23, 24	14	2	43, 44
16	9	25, 26	15	3	45, 46
17	10	27, 28, 29	16	4	47, 48, 49
18	11: 1-15	30, 31	17	5	50, 51, 52
		ECCL.		**2 THESS.**	
19	11:16-33	1, 2, 3	18	1	53, 54, 55
20	12	4, 5, 6	19	2	56, 57, 58
21	13	7, 8, 9	20	3	59, 60, 61
	GAL.			**1 TIM.**	
22	1	10, 11, 12	21	1	62, 63, 64
		SONG	22	2	65, 66
23	2	1, 2, 3			**JER.**
24	3	4, 5	23	3	1, 2
25	4	6, 7, 8	24	4	3, 4, 5
		IS.	25	5	6, 7, 8
26	5	1, 2	26	6	9, 10, 11
27	6	3, 4		**2 TIM.**	
	EPH.		27	1	12, 13, 14
28	1	5, 6	28	2	15, 16, 17
29	2	7, 8	29	3	18, 19
30	3	9, 10	30	4	20, 21
				TITUS	
			31	1	22, 23

METHOD 2 *(continued)*

NOVEMBER			DECEMBER		
Date	MORNING	EVENING	Date	MORNING	EVENING
	TITUS	JER.		2 PET.	EZEK.
1	2	24, 25, 26	1	3	40, 41
2	3	27, 28, 29		1 JOHN	
3	PHILEM.	30, 31	2	1	42, 43, 44
	HEB.		3	2	45, 46
4	1	32, 33	4	3	47, 48
5	2	34, 35, 36			DAN.
6	3	37, 38, 39	5	4	1, 2
7	4	40, 41, 42	6	5	3, 4
8	5	43, 44, 45	7	2 JOHN	5, 6, 7
9	6	46, 47	8	3 JOHN	8, 9, 10
10	7	48, 49	9	JUDE	11, 12
11	8	50		REV.	HOS.
12	9	51, 52	10	1	1, 2, 3, 4
		LAM.	11	2	5, 6, 7, 8
13	10: 1-18	1, 2	12	3	9, 10, 11
14	10:19-39	3, 4, 5	13	4	12, 13, 14
		EZEK.	14	5	JOEL
15	11: 1-19	1, 2			AMOS
16	11:20-40	3, 4	15	6	1, 2, 3
17	12	5, 6, 7	16	7	4, 5, 6
18	13	8, 9, 10	17	8	7, 8, 9
	JAMES		18	9	OBAD.
19	1	11, 12, 13	19	10	JON.
20	2	14, 15			MIC.
21	3	16, 17	20	11	1, 2, 3
22	4	18, 19	21	12	4, 5
23	5	20, 21	22	13	6, 7
	1 PET.		23	14	NAH.
24	1	22, 23	24	15	HAB.
25	2	24, 25, 26	25	16	ZEPH.
26	3	27, 28, 29	26	17	HAG.
27	4	30, 31, 32			ZECH.
28	5	33, 34	27	18	1, 2, 3, 4
	2 PET.		28	19	5, 6, 7, 8
29	1	35, 36	29	20	9, 10, 11, 12
30	2	37, 38, 39	30	21	13, 14
			31	22	MAL.

METHOD 3

(Bible in a Year, Cover to Cover, on a Consecutive Schedule)

WEEK 1	WEEK 5
Day 1: Genesis 1, 2	Day 1: Exodus 32–34
Day 2: Genesis 3–5	Day 2: Exodus 35–40
Day 3: Genesis 6–9	Day 3: Leviticus 1–3
Day 4: Genesis 10, 11	Day 4: Leviticus 4–7
Day 5: Genesis 12–14	Day 5: Leviticus 8–10
Day 6: Genesis 15–17	Day 6: Leviticus 11–15

WEEK 2	WEEK 6
Day 1: Genesis 18–20	Day 1: Leviticus 16, 17
Day 2: Genesis 21–24	Day 2: Leviticus 18–20
Day 3: Genesis 25, 26	Day 3: Leviticus 21–23
Day 4: Genesis 27–31	Day 4: Leviticus 24–27
Day 5: Genesis 32–36	Day 5: Numbers 1–4
Day 6: Genesis 37–40	Day 6: Numbers 5–8

WEEK 3	WEEK 7
Day 1: Genesis 41–44	Day 1: Numbers 9–12
Day 2: Genesis 45–47	Day 2: Numbers 13–16
Day 3: Genesis 48–50	Day 3: Numbers 17–20
Day 4: Exodus 1, 2	Day 4: Numbers 21–25
Day 5: Exodus 3–6	Day 5: Numbers 26–30
Day 6: Exodus 7–10	Day 6: Numbers 31–33

WEEK 4	WEEK 8
Day 1: Exodus 11–15	Day 1: Numbers 34–36
Day 2: Exodus 16–18	Day 2: Deuteronomy 1–4
Day 3: Exodus 19, 20	Day 3: Deuteronomy 5–7
Day 4: Exodus 21–24	Day 4: Deuteronomy 8–11
Day 5: Exodus 25–27	Day 5: Deuteronomy 12–16
Day 6: Exodus 28–31	Day 6: Deuteronomy 17–20

METHOD 3 *(continued)*

WEEK 9	**WEEK 13**
Day 1: Deuteronomy 21–26	Day 1: 2 Samuel 5–7
Day 2: Deuteronomy 27–30	Day 2: 2 Samuel 8–10
Day 3: Deuteronomy 31–34	Day 3: 2 Samuel 11–14
Day 4: Joshua 1–5	Day 4: 2 Samuel 15–18
Day 5: Joshua 6–8	Day 5: 2 Samuel 19, 20
Day 6: Joshua 9–12	Day 6: 2 Samuel 21–24
WEEK 10	**WEEK 14**
Day 1: Joshua 13–17	Day 1: 1 Kings 1–4
Day 2: Joshua 18–21	Day 2: 1 Kings 5–8
Day 3: Joshua 22–24	Day 3: 1 Kings 9–11
Day 4: Judges 1–5	Day 4: 1 Kings 12–16
Day 5: Judges 6–8	Day 5: 1 Kings 17–19
Day 6: Judges 9–12	Day 6: 1 Kings 20–22
WEEK 11	**WEEK 15**
Day 1: Judges 13–16	Day 1: 2 Kings 1–3
Day 2: Judges 17–21	Day 2: 2 Kings 4–8
Day 3: Ruth 1–4	Day 3: 2 Kings 9–12
Day 4: 1 Samuel 1–3	Day 4: 2 Kings 13–17
Day 5: 1 Samuel 4–8	Day 5: 2 Kings 18–21
Day 6: 1 Samuel 9–12	Day 6: 2 Kings 22–25
WEEK 12	**WEEK 16**
Day 1: 1 Samuel 13–15	Day 1: 1 Chronicles 1–9
Day 2: 1 Samuel 16–19	Day 2: 1 Chronicles 10–16
Day 3: 1 Samuel 20–23	Day 3: 1 Chronicles 17–21
Day 4: 1 Samuel 24–26	Day 4: 1 Chronicles 22–27
Day 5: 1 Samuel 27–31	Day 5: 1 Chronicles 28, 29
Day 6: 2 Samuel 1–4	Day 6: 2 Chronicles 1–5

METHOD 3 (continued)

WEEK 17 Day 1: 2 Chronicles 6–9 Day 2: 2 Chronicles 10–12 Day 3: 2 Chronicles 13–16 Day 4: 2 Chronicles 17–20 Day 5: 2 Chronicles 21–25 Day 6: 2 Chronicles 26–28	**WEEK 21** Day 1: Job 15–17 Day 2: Job 18, 19 Day 3: Job 20, 21 Day 4: Job 22–24 Day 5: Job 25–28 Day 6: Job 29–31
WEEK 18 Day 1: 2 Chronicles 29–32 Day 2: 2 Chronicles 33–36 Day 3: Ezra 1–3 Day 4: Ezra 4–6 Day 5: Ezra 7, 8 Day 6: Ezra 9, 10	**WEEK 22** Day 1: Job 32–34 Day 2: Job 35–37 Day 3: Job 38, 39 Day 4: Job 40–42 Day 5: Psalms 1–6 Day 6: Psalms 7–12
WEEK 19 Day 1: Nehemiah 1–3 Day 2: Nehemiah 4–7 Day 3: Nehemiah 8–10 Day 4: Nehemiah 11–13 Day 5: Esther 1, 2 Day 6: Esther 3, 4	**WEEK 23** Day 1: Psalms 13–18 Day 2: Psalms 19–24 Day 3: Psalms 25–30 Day 4: Psalms 31–35 Day 5: Psalms 36–41 Day 6: Psalms 42–49
WEEK 20 Day 1: Esther 5–7 Day 2: Esther 8–10 Day 3: Job 1–3 Day 4: Job 4–7 Day 5: Job 8–10 Day 6: Job 11–14	**WEEK 24** Day 1: Psalms 50–54 Day 2: Psalms 55–59 Day 3: Psalms 60–66 Day 4: Psalms 67–72 Day 5: Psalms 73–77 Day 6: Psalms 78–83

METHOD 3 *(continued)*

WEEK 25	**WEEK 29**
Day 1: Psalms 84–89	Day 1: Isaiah 5–8
Day 2: Psalms 90–97	Day 2: Isaiah 9–12
Day 3: Psalms 98–103	Day 3: Isaiah 13–16
Day 4: Psalms 104–106	Day 4: Isaiah 17–20
Day 5: Psalms 107–110	Day 5: Isaiah 21–23
Day 6: Psalms 111–118	Day 6: Isaiah 24–27
WEEK 26	**WEEK 30**
Day 1: Psalm 119	Day 1: Isaiah 28–30
Day 2: Psalms 120–127	Day 2: Isaiah 31–35
Day 3: Psalms 128–134	Day 3: Isaiah 36–39
Day 4: Psalms 135–139	Day 4: Isaiah 40–43
Day 5: Psalms 140–145	Day 5: Isaiah 44–48
Day 6: Psalms 146–150	Day 6: Isaiah 49–51
WEEK 27	**WEEK 31**
Day 1: Proverbs 1–4	Day 1: Isaiah 52–57
Day 2: Proverbs 5–9	Day 2: Isaiah 58–62
Day 3: Proverbs 10–13	Day 3: Isaiah 63–66
Day 4: Proverbs 14–17	Day 4: Jeremiah 1–3
Day 5: Proverbs 18–21	Day 5: Jeremiah 4–6
Day 6: Proverbs 22–24	Day 6: Jeremiah 7–10
WEEK 28	**WEEK 32**
Day 1: Proverbs 25–29	Day 1: Jeremiah 11–15
Day 2: Proverbs 30, 31	Day 2: Jeremiah 16–20
Day 3: Ecclesiastes 1–6	Day 3: Jeremiah 21–25
Day 4: Ecclesiastes 7–12	Day 4: Jeremiah 26–29
Day 5: Song of Solomon 1–8	Day 5: Jeremiah 30–33
Day 6: Isaiah 1–4	Day 6: Jeremiah 34–39

METHOD 3 *(continued)*

WEEK 33	**WEEK 37**
Day 1: Jeremiah 40−45	Day 1: Amos 1, 2
Day 2: Jeremiah 46−49	Day 2: Amos 3−5
Day 3: Jeremiah 50−52	Day 3: Amos 6, 7
Day 4: Lamentations 1−5	Day 4: Amos 8, 9
Day 5: Ezekiel 1−6	Day 5: Obadiah
Day 6: Ezekiel 7−11	Day 6: Jonah 1−4

WEEK 34	**WEEK 38**
Day 1: Ezekiel 12−15	Day 1: Micah 1, 2
Day 2: Ezekiel 16−19	Day 2: Micah 3−5
Day 3: Ezekiel 20−23	Day 3: Micah 6, 7
Day 4: Ezekiel 24−28	Day 4: Nahum 1−3
Day 5: Ezekiel 29−32	Day 5: Habakkuk 1−3
Day 6: Ezekiel 33−36	Day 6: Zephaniah 1−3

WEEK 35	**WEEK 39**
Day 1: Ezekiel 37−39	Day 1: Haggai 1, 2
Day 2: Ezekiel 40−43	Day 2: Zechariah 1, 2
Day 3: Ezekiel 44−48	Day 3: Zechariah 3, 4
Day 4: Daniel 1−3	Day 4: Zechariah 5, 6
Day 5: Daniel 4−6	Day 5: Zechariah 7, 8
Day 6: Daniel 7−12	Day 6: Zechariah 9−11

WEEK 36	**WEEK 40**
Day 1: Hosea 1−3	Day 1: Zechariah 12−14
Day 2: Hosea 4−6	Day 2: Malachi 1−4
Day 3: Hosea 7, 8	Day 3: Matthew 1−4
Day 4: Hosea 9−11	Day 4: Matthew 5−7
Day 5: Hosea 12−14	Day 5: Matthew 8−11
Day 6: Joel 1−3	Day 6: Matthew 12−15

METHOD 3 (continued)

WEEK 41	**WEEK 45**
Day 1: Matthew 16–19	Day 1: Acts 8, 9
Day 2: Matthew 20–25	Day 2: Acts 10–12
Day 3: Matthew 26–28	Day 3: Acts 13–15
Day 4: Mark 1–3	Day 4: Acts 16–18
Day 5: Mark 4–7	Day 5: Acts 19, 20
Day 6: Mark 8–10	Day 6: Acts 21–23
WEEK 42	**WEEK 46**
Day 1: Mark 11–13	Day 1: Acts 24–26
Day 2: Mark 14–16	Day 2: Acts 27, 28
Day 3: Luke 1–4	Day 3: Romans 1–3
Day 4: Luke 5–7	Day 4: Romans 4, 5
Day 5: Luke 8–11	Day 5: Romans 6–8
Day 6: Luke 12–14	Day 6: Romans 9–11
WEEK 43	**WEEK 47**
Day 1: Luke 15–18	Day 1: Romans 12–16
Day 2: Luke 19–21	Day 2: 1 Corinthians 1–6
Day 3: Luke 22–24	Day 3: 1 Corinthians 7–10
Day 4: John 1–4	Day 4: 1 Corinthians 11–14
Day 5: John 5–7	Day 5: 1 Corinthians 15, 16
Day 6: John 8–10	Day 6: 2 Corinthians 1–5
WEEK 44	**WEEK 48**
Day 1: John 11, 12	Day 1: 2 Corinthians 6–9
Day 2: John 13, 14	Day 2: 2 Corinthians 10–13
Day 3: John 15–17	Day 3: Galatians 1–6
Day 4: John 18–21	Day 4: Ephesians 1–6
Day 5: Acts 1–4	Day 5: Philippians 1–4
Day 6: Acts 5–7	Day 6: Colossians 1–4

METHOD 3 *(continued)*

WEEK 49	**WEEK 51**
Day 1: 1 Thessalonians 1–5	Day 1: 1 Peter 1–5
Day 2: 2 Thessalonians 1–3	Day 2: 2 Peter 1–3
Day 3: 1 Timothy 1–6	Day 3: 1 John 1–5
Day 4: 2 Timothy 1–4	Day 4: 2 John
Day 5: Titus 1–3	Day 5: 3 John
Day 6: Philemon	Day 6: Jude
WEEK 50	**WEEK 52**
Day 1: Hebrews 1, 2	Day 1: Revelation 1–5
Day 2: Hebrews 3, 4	Day 2: Revelation 6–9
Day 3: Hebrews 5–7	Day 3: Revelation 10–13
Day 4: Hebrews 8–10	Day 4: Revelation 14–16
Day 5: Hebrews 11–13	Day 5: Revelation 17–19
Day 6: James 1–5	Day 6: Revelation 20–22

METHOD 4
(New Testament in a Year)

WEEK 1	WEEK 5
Day 1: Matthew 1	Day 1: Matthew 27
Day 2: Matthew 2	Day 2: Matthew 28
Day 3: Matthew 3, 4	Day 3: Mark 1:1-20
Day 4: Matthew 5	Day 4: Mark 1:21-45
Day 5: Matthew 6	Day 5: Mark 2
Day 6: Matthew 7	Day 6: Mark 3:1-19
WEEK 2	**WEEK 6**
Day 1: Matthew 8	Day 1: Mark 3:20-35
Day 2: Matthew 9	Day 2: Mark 4:1-34
Day 3: Matthew 10	Day 3: Mark 4:35-5:20
Day 4: Matthew 11	Day 4: Mark 5:21-43
Day 5: Matthew 12	Day 5: Mark 6:1-29
Day 6: Matthew 13	Day 6: Mark 6:30-56
WEEK 3	**WEEK 7**
Day 1: Matthew 14	Day 1: Mark 7:1-30
Day 2: Matthew 15	Day 2: Mark 7:31-8:13
Day 3: Matthew 16	Day 3: Mark 8:14-38
Day 4: Matthew 17	Day 4: Mark 9:1-32
Day 5: Matthew 18, 19	Day 5: Mark 9:33-10:16
Day 6: Matthew 20	Day 6: Mark 10:17-52
WEEK 4	**WEEK 8**
Day 1: Matthew 21	Day 1: Mark 11:1-19
Day 2: Matthew 22	Day 2: Mark 11:20-12:12
Day 3: Matthew 23	Day 3: Mark 12:13-44
Day 4: Matthew 24	Day 4: Mark 13:1-31
Day 5: Matthew 25	Day 5: Mark 13:32-14:11
Day 6: Matthew 26	Day 6: Mark 14:12-42

METHOD 4 *(continued)*

WEEK 9	WEEK 13
Day 1: Mark 14:43-72	Day 1: Luke 20
Day 2: Mark 15:1-20	Day 2: Luke 21
Day 3: Mark 15:21-47	Day 3: Luke 22:1-38
Day 4: Mark 16	Day 4: Luke 22:39-71
Day 5: Luke 1:1-38	Day 5: Luke 23
Day 6: Luke 1:39-80	Day 6: Luke 24

WEEK 10	WEEK 14
Day 1: Luke 2	Day 1: John 1:1-34
Day 2: Luke 3	Day 2: John 1:35-52
Day 3: Luke 4	Day 3: John 2
Day 4: Luke 5	Day 4: John 3
Day 5: Luke 6	Day 5: John 4:1-42
Day 6: Luke 7	Day 6: John 4:43–5:16

WEEK 11	WEEK 15
Day 1: Luke 8	Day 1: John 5:17-47
Day 2: Luke 9	Day 2: John 6:1-21
Day 3: Luke 10	Day 3: John 6:22-71
Day 4: Luke 11	Day 4: John 7
Day 5: Luke 12	Day 5: John 8:1-30
Day 6: Luke 13	Day 6: John 8:31-59

WEEK 12	WEEK 16
Day 1: Luke 14	Day 1: John 9
Day 2: Luke 15	Day 2: John 10
Day 3: Luke 16	Day 3: John 11:1-45
Day 4: Luke 17	Day 4: John 11:46–12:19
Day 5: Luke 18	Day 5: John 12:20-50
Day 6: Luke 19	Day 6: John 13

METHOD 4 *(continued)*

WEEK 17	WEEK 21
Day 1: John 14	Day 1: Acts 20
Day 2: John 15	Day 2: Acts 21
Day 3: John 16	Day 3: Acts 22
Day 4: John 17	Day 4: Acts 23
Day 5: John 18	Day 5: Acts 24:1–25:12
Day 6: John 19	Day 6: Acts 25:13–26:32

WEEK 18	WEEK 22
Day 1: John 20	Day 1: Acts 27
Day 2: John 21	Day 2: Acts 28
Day 3: Acts 1	Day 3: Romans 1:1-17
Day 4: Acts 2	Day 4: Romans 1:18-32
Day 5: Acts 3	Day 5: Romans 2:1-16
Day 6: Acts 4	Day 6: Romans 2:17-29

WEEK 19	WEEK 23
Day 1: Acts 5, 6	Day 1: Romans 3:1-20
Day 2: Acts 7	Day 2: Romans 3:21-31
Day 3: Acts 8	Day 3: Romans 4:1-12
Day 4: Acts 9	Day 4: Romans 4:13-25
Day 5: Acts 10	Day 5: Romans 5:1-11
Day 6: Acts 11, 12	Day 6: Romans 5:12-21

WEEK 20	WEEK 24
Day 1: Acts 13	Day 1: Romans 6:1-11
Day 2: Acts 14	Day 2: Romans 6:12-23
Day 3: Acts 15	Day 3: Romans 7:1-12
Day 4: Acts 16	Day 4: Romans 7:13-25
Day 5: Acts 17:1–18:21	Day 5: Romans 8:1-11
Day 6: Acts 18:22–19:41	Day 6: Romans 8:12-25

METHOD 4 *(continued)*

WEEK 25	WEEK 29
Day 1: Romans 8:26-39	Day 1: 1 Corinthians 15:35-58
Day 2: Romans 9:1-29	Day 2: 1 Corinthians 16
Day 3: Romans 9:30–10:21	Day 3: 2 Corinthians 1:1–2:11
Day 4: Romans 11:1-10	Day 4: 2 Corinthians 2:12–3:18
Day 5: Romans 11:11-36	Day 5: 2 Corinthians 4
Day 6: Romans 12	Day 6: 2 Corinthians 5:1–6:2
WEEK 26	**WEEK 30**
Day 1: Romans 13	Day 1: 2 Corinthians 6:3–7:16
Day 2: Romans 14	Day 2: 2 Corinthians 8
Day 3: Romans 15:1-13	Day 3: 2 Corinthians 9
Day 4: Romans 15:14–16:27	Day 4: 2 Corinthians 10:1–11:15
Day 5: 1 Corinthians 1	Day 5: 2 Corinthians 11:16–12:10
Day 6: 1 Corinthians 2	Day 6: 2 Corinthians 12:11–13:14
WEEK 27	**WEEK 31**
Day 1: 1 Corinthians 3	Day 1: Galatians 1
Day 2: 1 Corinthians 4	Day 2: Galatians 2
Day 3: 1 Corinthians 5, 6	Day 3: Galatians 3:1-25
Day 4: 1 Corinthians 7	Day 4: Galatians 3:26–4:20
Day 5: 1 Corinthians 8	Day 5: Galatians 4:21–5:12
Day 6: 1 Corinthians 9	Day 6: Galatians 5:13-26
WEEK 28	**WEEK 32**
Day 1: 1 Corinthians 10:1–11:1	Day 1: Galatians 6
Day 2: 1 Corinthians 11:2-34	Day 2: Ephesians 1:1-14
Day 3: 1 Corinthians 12	Day 3: Ephesians 1:15–2:10
Day 4: 1 Corinthians 13	Day 4: Ephesians 2:11-22
Day 5: 1 Corinthians 14	Day 5: Ephesians 3
Day 6: 1 Corinthians 15:1-34	Day 6: Ephesians 4:1-16

METHOD 4 *(continued)*

WEEK 33	WEEK 37
Day 1: Ephesians 4:17—5:2	Day 1: 1 Timothy 2
Day 2: Ephesians 5:3-21	Day 2: 1 Timothy 3:1-13
Day 3: Ephesians 5:22—6:9	Day 3: 1 Timothy 3:14—4:10
Day 4: Ephesians 6:10-24	Day 4: 1 Timothy 4:11—5:8
Day 5: Philippians 1	Day 5: 1 Timothy 5:9—6:2
Day 6: Philippians 2:1-11	Day 6: 1 Timothy 6:3-21
WEEK 34	**WEEK 38**
Day 1: Philippians 2:12-30	Day 1: 2 Timothy 1:1-14
Day 2: Philippians 3:1—4:1	Day 2: 2 Timothy 1:15—2:7
Day 3: Philippians 4:2-23	Day 3: 2 Timothy 2:8-21
Day 4: Colossians 1:1-15	Day 4: 2 Timothy 2:22—3:9
Day 5: Colossians 1:16—2:5	Day 5: 2 Timothy 3:10—4:5
Day 6: Colossians 2:6-23	Day 6: 2 Timothy 4:6-22
WEEK 35	**WEEK 39**
Day 1: Colossians 3:1—4:1	Day 1: Titus 1
Day 2: Colossians 4:2-18	Day 2: Titus 2
Day 3: 1 Thessalonians 1	Day 3: Titus 3
Day 4: 1 Thessalonians 2:1-16	Day 4: Philemon
Day 5: 1 Thessalonians 2:17—3:13	Day 5: Hebrews 1
Day 6: 1 Thessalonians 4:1-12	Day 6: Hebrews 2
WEEK 36	**WEEK 40**
Day 1: 1 Thessalonians 4:13—5:11	Day 1: Hebrews 3
Day 2: 1 Thessalonians 5:12-28	Day 2: Hebrews 4:1-13
Day 3: 2 Thessalonians 1	Day 3: Hebrews 4:14—5:10
Day 4: 2 Thessalonians 2	Day 4: Hebrews 5:11—6:12
Day 5: 2 Thessalonians 3	Day 5: Hebrews 6:13—7:10
Day 6: 1 Timothy 1	Day 6: Hebrews 7:11-28

METHOD 4 *(continued)*

WEEK 41	WEEK 45
Day 1: Hebrews 8	Day 1: 1 Peter 4:1-11
Day 2: Hebrews 9:1-14	Day 2: 1 Peter 4:12-19
Day 3: Hebrews 9:15-28	Day 3: 1 Peter 5
Day 4: Hebrews 10:1-18	Day 4: 2 Peter 1:1-11
Day 5: Hebrews 10:19-39	Day 5: 2 Peter 1:12-21
Day 6: Hebrews 11:1-16	Day 6: 2 Peter 2:1-11

WEEK 42	WEEK 46
Day 1: Hebrews 11:17-40	Day 1: 2 Peter 2:12-22
Day 2: Hebrews 12:1-13	Day 2: 2 Peter 3:1-10
Day 3: Hebrews 12:14-29	Day 3: 2 Peter 3:11-18
Day 4: Hebrews 13:1-14	Day 4: 1 John 1
Day 5: Hebrews 13:15-25	Day 5: 1 John 2:1-17
Day 6: James 1:1-18	Day 6: 1 John 2:18-29

WEEK 43	WEEK 47
Day 1: James 1:19-27	Day 1: 1 John 3:1-10
Day 2: James 2:1-13	Day 2: 1 John 3:11—4:6
Day 3: James 2:14-26	Day 3: 1 John 4:7-21
Day 4: James 3	Day 4: 1 John 5:1-12
Day 5: James 4	Day 5: 1 John 5:13-21
Day 6: James 5	Day 6: 2 John

WEEK 44	WEEK 48
Day 1: 1 Peter 1:1-12	Day 1: 3 John
Day 2: 1 Peter 1:13—2:3	Day 2: Jude
Day 3: 1 Peter 2:4-12	Day 3: Revelation 1:1-8
Day 4: 1 Peter 2:13-25	Day 4: Revelation 1:9-20
Day 5: 1 Peter 3:1-12	Day 5: Revelation 2:1-11
Day 6: 1 Peter 3:13-22	Day 6: Revelation 2:12-29

METHOD 4 *(continued)*

WEEK 49	WEEK 51
Day 1: Revelation 3:1-13	Day 1: Revelation 14
Day 2: Revelation 3:14-22	Day 2: Revelation 15
Day 3: Revelation 4	Day 3: Revelation 16
Day 4: Revelation 5	Day 4: Revelation 17
Day 5: Revelation 6	Day 5: Revelation 18
Day 6: Revelation 7	Day 6: Revelation 19:1-10
WEEK 50	**WEEK 52**
Day 1: Revelation 8	Day 1: Revelation 19:11-21
Day 2: Revelation 9	Day 2: Revelation 20
Day 3: Revelation 10	Day 3: Revelation 21:1-8
Day 4: Revelation 11	Day 4: Revelation 21:9-27
Day 5: Revelation 12	Day 5: Revelation 22:1-9
Day 6: Revelation 13	Day 6: Revelation 22:10-21

METHOD 8
(31 Key Psalms Per Month)

1.	Psalm 1	12.	Psalm 34	22.	Psalm 100
2.	Psalm 8	13.	Psalm 37	23.	Psalm 103
3.	Psalm 15	14.	Psalm 67	24.	Psalm 111
4.	Psalm 16	15.	Psalm 73	25.	Psalm 127
5.	Psalm 19	16.	Psalm 84	26.	Psalm 130
6.	Psalm 23	17.	Psalm 90	27.	Psalm 131
7.	Psalm 25	18.	Psalm 91	28.	Psalm 139
8.	Psalm 27	19.	Psalm 92	29.	Psalm 145
9.	Psalm 29	20.	Psalm 95	30.	Psalm 147
10.	Psalm 32	21.	Psalm 96	31.	Psalm 148
11.	Psalm 33				

How to Use the Memory Verse Guide

The Memory Verse Guide offers three levels of topically arranged Bible verses. Each level contains 52 passages, so that you can learn a level in one year at the rate of one passage per week.

Level One provides you with foundational verses on ten major areas of the Christian walk:

1. Salvation
2. Assurance of salvation
3. Spiritual life
4. Prayer
5. Bible study
6. God's will
7. Evangelism
8. Spiritual gifts
9. Spiritual warfare
10. Stewardship

Level Two centers around the themes of loving God, self, and others:

1. Loving God completely (13 passages)
2. Loving self correctly (13 passages)
3. Loving others compassionately (26 passages)
   a. Husband and wife
   b. Parent and child
   c. Employee and employer
   d. Christian and Christian
   e. Christian and the world
   f. Christian and creation

Level Three is structured around the ten areas of Christian doctrine. Each of these ten doctrines is subdivided into four categories:

1. The doctrine of the Bible
   a. Revelation
   b. Inspiration
   c. Illumination
   d. Interpretation

2. The doctrine of God
   a. Existence
   b. Attributes
   c. Sovereignty
   d. Trinity

3. The doctrine of Christ
   a. Deity
   b. Humanity
   c. Resurrection
   d. Return

4. The doctrine of the Holy Spirit
   a. Deity
   b. Work in salvation
   c. Filling
   d. Spiritual gifts

5. The doctrine of angels
   a. Angels
   b. Demons
   c. Satan
   d. Believers' defense

6. The doctrine of man
   a. Origin
   b. Purpose
   c. Nature
   d. Fall

7. The doctrine of sin
   a. Definition
   b. Result
   c. Provision
   d. Victory

8. The doctrine of salvation
   a. Basis
   b. Results
   c. Benefits
   d. Assurance

9. The doctrine of the church
   a. Local church
   b. Universal church
   c. Edification
   d. Evangelism

10. The doctrine of future things
    a. Second Coming
    b. Judgment of believers
    c. Judgment of unbelievers
    d. Heaven

Suggestions

1. This is a systematic arrangement, and it is best to memorize the verses in the order in which they appear in this guide.
2. Consider committing yourself to mastering Level One. These are the core verses you should review and retain, even if you later learn and forget other verses.
3. Set specific and realistic goals. At the rate of one passage per week, it will take you a year. Some people may want to learn Level One in six months (two passages per week). Others may take two years (one passage every two weeks).
4. Review is essential to retention, and it plays an increasingly important role with every new verse you learn. Be sure to review what you have memorized so that it will not gradually slip away from you. The more you have learned, the more important a methodical program of review will become.

Level One: The Christian Walk

1. Salvation

For all have sinned and fall short of the glory of God.
Rom. 3:23

For the wages of sin is death, but the gift of God is eternal life in Christ Jesus our Lord.　　Rom. 6:23

For God so loved the world that He gave His only begotten Son, that whoever believes in Him should not perish but have everlasting life.　　John 3:16

But as many as received Him, to them He gave the right to become children of God, to those who believe in His name.　　John 1:12

Not by works of righteousness which we have done, but according to His mercy He saved us, through the washing of regeneration and renewing of the Holy Spirit.　　Titus 3:5

For He made Him who knew no sin to be sin for us, that we might become the righteousness of God in Him.　　2 Cor. 5:21

2. Assurance of Salvation

Most assuredly, I say to you, he who hears My word and believes in Him who sent Me has everlasting life, and shall not come into judgment, but has passed from death into life.　　John 5:24

My sheep hear My voice, and I know them, and they follow Me. And I give them eternal life, and they shall never perish; neither shall anyone snatch them out of My hand. My Father, who has given them to Me, is greater than all; and no one is able to snatch them out of My Father's hand.   John 10:27-29

I am the resurrection and the life. He who believes in Me, though he may die, he shall live. And whoever lives and believes in Me shall never die.

John 11:25, 26

Blessed be the God and Father of our Lord Jesus Christ, who according to His abundant mercy has begotten us again to a living hope through the resurrection of Jesus Christ from the dead, to an inheritance incorruptible and undefiled and that does not fade away, reserved in heaven for you, who are kept by the power of God through faith for salvation ready to be revealed in the last time.   1 Pet. 1:3-5

For I am persuaded that neither death nor life, nor angels nor principalities nor powers, nor things present nor things to come, nor height nor depth, nor any other created thing, shall be able to separate us from the love of God which is in Christ Jesus our Lord.   Rom. 8:38, 39

3. Spiritual Life

Therefore, if anyone is in Christ, he is a new creation; old things have passed away; behold, all things have become new.   2 Cor. 5:17

He who has My commandments and keeps them, it is he who loves Me. And he who loves Me will be loved by My Father, and I will love him and manifest Myself to him. John 14:21

Abide in Me, and I in you. As the branch cannot bear fruit of itself, unless it abides in the vine, neither can you, unless you abide in Me. I am the vine, you are the branches. He who abides in Me, and I in him, bears much fruit; for without Me you can do nothing. John 15:4, 5

Therefore, my beloved, as you have always obeyed, not as in my presence only, but now much more in my absence, work out your own salvation with fear and trembling; for it is God who works in you both to will and to do for His good pleasure. Phil. 2:12, 13

Likewise you also, reckon yourselves to be dead indeed to sin, but alive to God in Christ Jesus our Lord. Rom. 6:11

No temptation has overtaken you except such as is common to man; but God is faithful, who will not allow you to be tempted beyond what you are able, but with the temptation will also make the way of escape, that you may be able to bear it. 1 Cor. 10:13

4. Prayer

Ask, and it will be given to you; seek, and you will find; knock, and it will be opened to you. For everyone who asks receives, and he who seeks finds, and to him who knocks it will be opened.

Matt. 7:7, 8

If you keep My commandments, you will abide in My love, just as I have kept My Father's commandments and abide in His love.

John 15:10

Now this is the confidence which we have in Him, that if we ask anything according to His will, He hears us.

1 John 5:14

Be anxious for nothing, but in everything by prayer and supplication, with thanksgiving, let your requests be made known to God; and the peace of God, which surpasses all understanding, will guard your hearts and minds through Christ Jesus.

Phil. 4:6, 7

If we confess our sins, He is faithful and just to forgive us our sins and to cleanse us from all unrighteousness.

1 John 1:9

5. Bible Study

All Scripture is given by inspiration of God, and is profitable for doctrine, for reproof, for correction, for instruction in righteousness, that the man of God may be complete, thoroughly equipped for every good work.

2 Tim. 3:16, 17

For the word of God is living and powerful, and sharper than any two-edged sword, piercing even to the division of soul and spirit, and of joints and

147

marrow, and is a discerner of the thoughts and
intents of the heart. Heb. 4:12

But his delight is in the law of the LORD,
And in His law he meditates day and night.

Ps. 1:2

This Book of the Law shall not depart from your
mouth, but you shall meditate in it day and night,
that you may observe to do according to all that is
written in it. For then you will make your way
prosperous, and then you will have good success.

Josh. 1:8

But be doers of the word, and not hearers only,
deceiving yourselves. James 1:22

6. God's Will

Trust in the LORD with all your heart,
And lean not on your own understanding;
In all your ways acknowledge Him,
And He shall direct your paths. Prov. 3:5, 6

I beseech you therefore, brethren, by the mercies of
God, that you present your bodies a living sacrifice,
holy, acceptable to God, which is your reasonable
service. And do not be conformed to this world, but
be transformed by the renewing of your mind, that
you may prove what is that good and acceptable and
perfect will of God. Rom. 12:1, 2

For we are His workmanship, created in Christ Jesus
for good works, which God prepared beforehand,
that we should walk in them. Eph. 2:10

He who says he abides in Him ought himself also to walk just as He walked.   1 John 2:6

And we know that all things work together for good to those who love God, to those who are the called according to His purpose.   Rom. 8:28

7. Evangelism

All authority has been given to Me in heaven and on earth. Go therefore and make disciples of all the nations, baptizing them in the name of the Father and of the Son and of the Holy Spirit, teaching them to observe all things that I have commanded you; and lo, I am with you always, even to the end of the age.
                    Matt. 28:18-20

But sanctify the Lord God in your hearts, and always be ready to give a defense to everyone who asks you a reason for the hope that is in you, with meekness and fear.   1 Pet. 3:15

Walk in wisdom toward those who are outside, redeeming the time. Let your speech always be with grace, seasoned with salt, that you may know how you ought to answer each one.   Col. 4:5, 6

He who has the Son has life; he who does not have the Son of God does not have life.
                    1 John 5:12

And for me, that utterance may be given to me, that I may open my mouth boldly to make known the mystery of the gospel.   Eph. 6:19

8. Spiritual Gifts

For as we have many members in one body, but all the members do not have the same function, so we, being many, are one body in Christ, and individually members of one another. Rom. 12:4, 5

And the things that you have heard from me among many witnesses, commit these to faithful men who will be able to teach others also. 2 Tim. 2:2

And He Himself gave some to be apostles, some prophets, some evangelists, and some pastors and teachers, for the equipping of the saints for the work of ministry, for the edifying of the body of Christ.
Eph. 4:11, 12

As each one has received a gift, minister it to one another, as good stewards of the manifold grace of God. 1 Pet. 4:10

Therefore, as we have opportunity, let us do good to all, especially to those who are of the household of faith. Gal. 6:10

9. Spiritual Warfare

Alert

Be sober, be vigilant; because your adversary the devil walks about like a roaring lion, seeking whom he may devour. 1 Pet. 5:8

Armor

Therefore take up the whole armor of God, that you may be able to withstand in the evil day, and having

done all, to stand. Stand therefore, having girded your
waist with truth, having put on the breastplate of
righteousness, and having shod your feet with the
preparation of the gospel of peace.   Eph. 6:13-15

Above all, taking the shield of faith with which you
will be able to quench all the fiery darts of the
wicked one. And take the helmet of salvation, and
the sword of the Spirit, which is the word of God.
                                              Eph. 6:16, 17

Praying always with all prayer and supplication in the
Spirit, being watchful to this end with all perseverance and supplication for all the saints.
                                                  Eph. 6:18

Resist

Therefore submit to God. Resist the devil and he will
flee from you.   James 4:7

10. Stewardship

But seek first the kingdom of God and His righteousness, and all these things shall be added to you.
                                                 Matt. 6:33

No servant can serve two masters; for either he will
hate the one and love the other, or else he will be
loyal to the one and despise the other. You cannot
serve God and mammon.   Luke 16:13

Honor the LORD with your possessions,
And with the firstfruits of all your increase.
                                                  Prov. 3:9

151

Let your conduct be without covetousness; be content with such things as you have. For He Himself has said, "I will never leave you nor forsake you."   Heb. 13:5

And my God shall supply all your need according to His riches in glory by Christ Jesus.   Phil. 4:19

Level Two: Loving God, Self, and Others

1. Loving God Completely

You shall love the LORD your God with all your heart, and with all your soul, and with all your strength.
                                               Deut. 6:5

But those who wait on the LORD
Shall renew their strength;
They shall mount up with wings like eagles,
They shall run and not be weary,
They shall walk and not faint.   Is. 40:31

"You shall love the LORD your God with all your heart, with all your soul, and with all your mind." This is the first and great commandment. And the second is like it: "You shall love your neighbor as yourself." On these two commandments hang all the Law and the Prophets.   Matt. 22:37-40

If anyone desires to come after Me, let him deny himself, and take up his cross daily, and follow Me.
                                               Luke 9:23

Peace I leave with you, My peace I give to you; not as the world gives do I give to you. Let not your heart be troubled, neither let it be afraid.

John 14:27

There is therefore now no condemnation to those who are in Christ Jesus, who do not walk according to the flesh, but according to the Spirit.

Rom. 8:1

I say then: Walk in the Spirit, and you shall not fulfill the lust of the flesh.

Gal. 5:16

But the fruit of the Spirit is love, joy, peace, longsuffering, kindness, goodness, faithfulness, gentleness, self-control. Against such there is no law.

Gal. 5:22, 23

Do not be deceived, God is not mocked; for whatever a man sows, that he will also reap.

Gal. 6:7

For to me, to live is Christ, and to die is gain.

Phil. 1:21

Now faith is the substance of things hoped for, the evidence of things not seen. But without faith it is impossible to please Him, for he who comes to God must believe that He is, and that He is a rewarder of those who diligently seek Him.

Heb. 11:1, 6

God resists the proud,
But gives grace to the humble.

Therefore humble yourselves under the mighty hand of God, that He may exalt you in due time, casting all your care upon Him, for He cares for you.

1 Pet. 5:5-7

Behold, I stand at the door and knock. If anyone hears My voice and opens the door, I will come in to him and dine with him, and he with Me.   Rev. 3:20

2. Loving Self Correctly

This being so, I myself always strive to have a conscience without offense toward God and men.

Acts 24:16

Knowing this, that our old man was crucified with Him, that the body of sin might be done away with, that we should no longer be slaves of sin.

Rom. 6:6

For I delight in the law of God according to the inward man.   Rom. 7:22

Or do you not know that your body is the temple of the Holy Spirit who is in you, whom you have from God, and you are not your own? For you were bought at a price; therefore glorify God in your body and in your spirit, which are God's.   1 Cor. 6:19, 20

For our light affliction, which is but for a moment, is working for us a far more exceeding and eternal weight of glory, while we do not look at the things which are seen, but at the things which are not seen. For the things which are seen are temporary, but the things which are not seen are eternal.

2 Cor. 4:17, 18

I have been crucified with Christ; it is no longer I who live, but Christ lives in me; and the life which I now live in the flesh I live by faith in the Son of God, who loved me, and gave Himself for me.

Gal. 2:20

And that you put on the new man which was created according to God, in true righteousness and holiness.

Eph. 4:24

For our citizenship is in heaven, from which we also eagerly wait for the Savior, the Lord Jesus Christ, who will transform our lowly body that it may be conformed to His glorious body, according to the working by which He is able to subdue all things to Himself.

Phil. 3:20, 21

Finally, brethren, whatever things are true, whatever things are noble, whatever things are just, whatever things are pure, whatever things are lovely, whatever things are of good report, if there is any virtue and if there is anything praiseworthy—meditate on these things. The things which you learned and received and heard and saw in me, these do, and the God of peace will be with you.

Phil. 4:8, 9

If then you were raised with Christ, seek those things which are above, where Christ is, sitting at the right hand of God. Set your mind on things above, not on things on the earth. For you died, and your life is hidden with Christ in God. When Christ who is our life appears, then you also will appear with Him in glory.

Col. 3:1-4

Let the word of Christ dwell in you richly in all wisdom, teaching and admonishing one another in psalms and hymns and spiritual songs, singing with grace in your hearts to the Lord.   Col. 3:16

For we do not have a High Priest who cannot sympathize with our weaknesses, but was in all points tempted as we are, yet without sin. Let us therefore come boldly to the throne of grace, that we may obtain mercy and find grace to help in time of need.   Heb. 4:15, 16

Therefore, gird up the loins of your mind, be sober, and rest your hope fully upon the grace that is to be brought to you at the revelation of Jesus Christ.
                                   1 Pet. 1:13

3. Loving Others Compassionately

Husband and wife

Therefore a man shall leave his father and mother and be joined to his wife, and they shall become one flesh.   Gen. 2:24

Husbands, love your wives, just as Christ also loved the church and gave Himself for her.
                                   Eph. 5:25

Wives, likewise, be submissive to your own husbands, that even if some do not obey the word, they, without a word, may be won by the conduct of their wives, when they observe your chaste conduct accompanied by fear.   1 Pet. 3:1, 2

Husbands, likewise, dwell with them with
understanding, giving honor to the wife, as to the
weaker vessel, and as being heirs together of the
grace of life, that your prayers may not be hindered.

1 Pet. 3:7

Parent and child

And these words, which I command you today shall
be in your heart. You shall teach them diligently to
your children, and shall talk of them when you sit in
your house, when you walk by the way, when you lie
down, and when you rise up.   Deut. 6:6, 7

Train up a child in the way he should go,
And when he is old he will not depart from it.

Prov. 22:6

And you, fathers, do not provoke your children to
wrath, but bring them up in the training and
admonition of the Lord.   Eph. 6:4

Employee and employer

Therefore, whether you eat or drink, or whatever you
do, do all to the glory of God.   1 Cor. 10:31

And whatever you do, do it heartily, as to the Lord
and not to men, knowing that from the Lord you will
receive the reward of the inheritance; for you serve
the Lord Christ.   Col. 3:23, 24

Masters, give your bondservants what is just and
fair, knowing that you also have a Master in heaven.

Col. 4:1

Christian and Christian

A new commandment I give to you, that you love one another; as I have loved you, that you also love one another. By this all will know that you are My disciples, if you have love for one another.

John 13:34, 35

And be kind to one another, tenderhearted, forgiving one another, even as God in Christ forgave you.

Eph. 4:32

Submitting to one another in the fear of God.

Eph. 5:21

Let nothing be done through selfish ambition or conceit, but in lowliness of mind let each esteem others better than himself. Let each of you look out not only for his own interests, but also for the interests of others.

Phil. 2:3, 4

Therefore, as the elect of God, holy and beloved, put on tender mercies, kindness, humility, meekness, longsuffering; bearing with one another, and forgiving one another, if anyone has a complaint against another; even as Christ forgave you, so you also must do.

Col. 3:12, 13

So then, my beloved brethren, let every man be swift to hear, slow to speak, slow to wrath; for the wrath of man does not produce the righteousness of God.

James 1:19, 20

Christian and the world

Non-Christian

Let your light so shine before men, that they may see your good works and glorify your Father in heaven.

Matt. 5:16

Therefore, whatever you want men to do to you, do also to them, for this is the Law and the Prophets.

Matt. 7:12

For even the Son of Man did not come to be served, but to serve, and to give His life a ransom for many.

Mark 10:45

Therefore I exhort first of all that supplications, prayers, intercessions, and giving of thanks be made for all men.

1 Tim. 2:1

World system

World

Adulterers and adulteresses! Do you not know that friendship with the world is enmity with God? Whoever therefore wants to be a friend of the world makes himself an enemy of God.

James 4:4

Flesh

Do not love the world or the things in the world. If anyone loves the world, the love of the Father is not in him. For all that is in the world—the lust of the flesh, the lust of the eyes, and the pride of life—is not of the Father but is of the world.

1 John 2:15, 16

Devil

You are of God, little children, and have overcome them, because He who is in you is greater than he who is in the world.   1 John 4:4

Christian and creation

Then God blessed them, and God said to them, "Be fruitful and multiply; fill the earth and subdue it; have dominion over the fish of the sea, over the birds of the air, and over every living thing that moves on the earth."   Gen. 1:28

O LORD, our Lord,
How excellent is Your name in all the earth,
Who have set Your glory above the heavens!

        Ps. 8:1

The heavens declare the glory of God;
And the firmament shows His handiwork.

        Ps. 19:1

Level Three: Christian Doctrine

Some of the best verses for Christian doctrine have already appeared in Level One and Level Two. In these cases, alternative verses have been selected for Level Three.

1. The Doctrine of the Bible

Revelation

God, who at various times and in various ways spoke in time past to the fathers by the prophets, has in

160

these last days spoken to us by His Son, whom He has appointed heir of all things, through whom also He made the worlds.   Heb. 1:1, 2

Inspiration

For prophecy never came by the will of man, but holy men of God spoke as they were moved by the Holy Spirit.   2 Pet. 1:21

Illumination

Now we have received, not the spirit of the world, but the Spirit who is from God, that we might know the things that have been freely given to us by God.
                                        1 Cor. 2:12

Interpretation

Be diligent to present yourself approved to God, a worker who does not need to be ashamed, rightly dividing the word of truth.   2 Tim. 2:15

2. The Doctrine of God

Existence

For the wrath of God is revealed from heaven against all ungodliness and unrighteousness of men, who suppress the truth in unrighteousness, because what may be known of God is manifest in them, for God has shown it to them. For since the creation of the world His invisible attributes are clearly seen, being understood by the things that are made, even His eternal power and Godhead, so that they are without excuse.   Rom. 1:18, 20

Attributes

Omnipresence

If I ascend into heaven, You are there;
If I make my bed in hell, behold, You are there.

Ps. 139:8

Omniscience

For there is not a word on my tongue,
But behold, O LORD,
You know it altogether.

Ps. 139:4

Omnipotence

I know that You can do everything,
And that no purpose of Yours can be withheld
from You.

Job 42:2

Love

He who does not love does not know God, for God is
love.

1 John 4:8

Justice

The fear of the LORD is clean, enduring forever;
The judgments of the LORD are true and righteous
altogether.

Ps. 19:9

Holiness

But the LORD of hosts shall be exalted in judgment,
And God who is holy shall be hallowed in
righteousness.

Is. 5:16

Immutability

Every good gift and every perfect gift is from above,
and comes down from the Father of lights, with
whom there is no variation or shadow of turning.

James 1:17

Truthfulness

I am the way, the truth, and the life. No one comes
to the Father except through Me.   John 14:6

Sovereignty

For I know that the LORD is great,
And our Lord is above all gods.
Whatever the LORD pleases He does,
In heaven and in earth,
In the seas and in all deep places.   Ps. 135:5, 6

Trinity

Hear, O Israel: The LORD our God, the LORD is one!
                                           Deut. 6:4

The grace of the Lord Jesus Christ, and the love of
God, and the communion of the Holy Spirit, be with
you all.   2 Cor. 13:14

3. The Doctrine of Christ

Deity

In the beginning was the Word, and the Word was
with God, and the Word was God.   John 1:1

Humanity

And the Word became flesh and dwelt among us, and
we beheld His glory, the glory as of the only begotten
of the Father, full of grace and truth.   John 1:14

Resurrection

And declared to be the Son of God with power
according to the Spirit of holiness, by the
resurrection from the dead.   Rom. 1:4

Return

Looking for the blessed hope and glorious appearing
of our great God and Savior Jesus Christ.

Titus 2:13

4. The Doctrine of the Holy Spirit

Deity

Where can I go from Your Spirit?
Or where can I flee from Your presence?

Ps. 139:7

Work in salvation

Conviction

And when He has come, He will convict the world of
sin, and of righteousness, and of judgment: of sin,
because they do not believe in Me; of righteousness,
because I go to My Father and you see Me no more;
of judgment, because the ruler of this world is
judged.   John 16:8-11

Regeneration

That which is born of the flesh is flesh, and that
which is born of the Spirit is spirit. Do not marvel
that I said to you, "You must be born again."

John 3:6, 7

Indwelling

But you are not in the flesh but in the Spirit, if
indeed the Spirit of God dwells in you. Now if anyone
does not have the Spirit of Christ, he is not His.

Rom. 8:9

Baptism

For by one Spirit we were all baptized into one body — whether Jews or Greeks, whether slaves or free — and have all been made to drink into one Spirit.
1 Cor. 12:13

Sealing

In Him you also trusted, after you heard the word of truth, the gospel of your salvation; in whom also, having believed, you were sealed with the Holy Spirit of promise, who is the guarantee of our inheritance until the redemption of the purchased possession, to the praise of His glory.
Eph. 1:13, 14

Filling

And do not be drunk with wine, in which is dissipation; but be filled with the Spirit.
Eph. 5:18

Spiritual gifts

There are diversities of gifts, but the same Spirit. But one and the same Spirit works all these things, distributing to each one individually as He wills.
1 Cor. 12:4, 11

5. The Doctrine of Angels

Angels

Are they not all ministering spirits sent forth to minister for those who will inherit salvation?
Heb. 1:14

Demons

And angels who did not keep their proper domain, but left their own abode, He has reserved in ever-

165

lasting chains under darkness for the judgment of the
great day. Jude 6

Satan

You are of your father the devil, and the desires of
your father you want to do. He was a murderer from
the beginning, and does not stand in the truth,
because there is no truth in him. When he speaks a
lie, he speaks from his own resources, for he is a liar
and the father of it. John 8:44

Believers' defense

For though we walk in the flesh, we do not war
according to the flesh. For the weapons of our
warfare are not carnal but mighty in God for pulling
down strongholds, casting down arguments and every
high thing that exalts itself against the knowledge of
God, bringing every thought into captivity to the
obedience of Christ. 2 Cor. 10:3-5

6. The Doctrine of Man

Origin

So God created man in His own image; in the image
of God He created him; male and female He created
them. Gen. 1:27

Purpose

In Him also we have obtained an inheritance, being
predestined according to the purpose of Him who
works all things according to the counsel of His will,
that we who first trusted in Christ should be to the
praise of His glory. Eph. 1:11, 12

Nature

Now may the God of peace Himself sanctify you completely; and may your whole spirit, soul, and body be preserved blameless at the coming of our Lord Jesus Christ.   1 Thess. 5:23

Fall

Therefore, just as through one man sin entered the world, and death through sin, and thus death spread to all men, because all sinned.   Rom. 5:12

7. The Doctrine of Sin

Definition

Whoever commits sin also commits lawlessness, and sin is lawlessness.   1 John 3:4

Result

And you He made alive, who were dead in trespasses and sins, in which you once walked according to the course of this world, according to the prince of the power of the air, the spirit who now works in the sons of disobedience, among whom also we all once conducted ourselves in the lusts of our flesh, fulfilling the desires of the flesh and of the mind, and were by nature children of wrath, just as the others.

Eph. 2:1-3

Provision

For Christ also suffered once for sins, the just for the unjust, that He might bring us to God, being put to death in the flesh but made alive by the Spirit.

1 Pet. 3:18

Victory

Therefore do not let sin reign in your mortal body, that you should obey it in its lusts. And do not present your members as instruments of unrighteousness to sin, but present yourselves to God as being alive from the dead, and your members as instruments of righteousness to God.   Rom. 6:12, 13

8. The Doctrine of Salvation

Basis

For by grace you have been saved through faith, and that not of yourselves; it is the gift of God, not of works, lest anyone should boast.   Eph. 2:8, 9

Results

Therefore, having been justified by faith, we have peace with God through our Lord Jesus Christ.

Rom. 5:1

Benefits

The thief does not come except to steal, and to kill, and to destroy. I have come that they may have life, and that they may have it more abundantly.

John 10:10

Assurance

These things I have written to you who believe in the name of the Son of God, that you may know that you have eternal life, and that you may continue to believe in the name of the Son of God.

1 John 5:13

9. The Doctrine of the Church

Local church

Therefore take heed to yourselves and to all the flock, among which the Holy Spirit has made you overseers, to shepherd the church of God which He purchased with His own blood.   Acts 20:28

Universal church

And He is the head of the body, the church, who is the beginning, the firstborn from the dead, that in all things He may have the preeminence.   Col. 1:18

Edification

Him we preach, warning every man and teaching every man in all wisdom, that we may present every man perfect in Christ Jesus.   Col. 1:28

Evangelism

Go into all the world and preach the gospel to every creature.   Mark 16:15

10. The Doctrine of Future Things

Second Coming

For the Son of Man will come in the glory of His Father with His angels, and then He will reward each according to his works.   Matt. 16:27

Judgment of believers

For we must all appear before the judgment seat of Christ, that each one may receive the things done in

the body, according to what he has done, whether
good or bad.   2 Cor. 5:10

Judgment of unbelievers

And anyone not found written in the Book of Life was
cast into the lake of fire.   Rev. 20:15

Heaven

In My Father's house are many mansions; if it were
not so, I would have told you. I go to prepare a place
for you. And if I go and prepare a place for you, I will
come again and receive you to Myself; that where I
am, there you may be also.   John 14:2, 3

Memory Verses in Biblical Order

Genesis 1:27

Genesis 1:28

Genesis 2:24

Deuteronomy 6:4

Deuteronomy 6:5

Deuteronomy 6:6, 7

Joshua 1:8

Job 42:2

Psalm 1:2

Psalm 8:1

Psalm 19:1

Psalm 19:9

Psalm 135:5, 6

Psalm 139:4

Psalm 139:7

Psalm 139:8

Proverbs 3:5, 6

Proverbs 3:9

Proverbs 22:6

Isaiah 5:16

Isaiah 40:31

Matthew 5:16

Matthew 6:33

Matthew 7:7, 8

Matthew 7:12

Matthew 16:27

Matthew 22:37-40

Matthew 28:18-20

Mark 10:45

Mark 16:15

Luke 9:23

Luke 16:13

John 1:1

John 1:12

John 1:14

John 3:6, 7

John 3:16

John 5:24

John 8:44

John 10:10

John 10:27-29

John 11:25, 26

John 13:34, 35

John 14:2, 3

John 14:6

John 14:21

John 14:27

John 15:4, 5

John 15:10

John 16:8-11

Acts 20:28

Acts 24:16

Romans 1:4

Romans 1:18-20

Romans 3:23

Romans 5:1

Romans 5:12

Romans 6:6

Romans 6:11

Romans 6:12, 13

Romans 6:23

Romans 7:22

Romans 8:1

Romans 8:9

Romans 8:28

Romans 8:38, 39

Romans 12:1, 2

Romans 12:4, 5

1 Corinthians 2:12

1 Corinthians 6:19, 20

1 Corinthians 10:13

1 Corinthians 10:31

1 Corinthians 12:4, 11

1 Corinthians 12:13

2 Corinthians 4:17, 18

2 Corinthians 5:10

2 Corinthians 5:17

2 Corinthians 5:21

2 Corinthians 10:3-5

2 Corinthians 13:14

Galatians 2:20

Galatians 5:16

Galatians 5:22, 23

Galatians 6:7

Galatians 6:10

Ephesians 1:11, 12

Ephesians 1:13, 14

Ephesians 2:1-3

Ephesians 2:8, 9

Ephesians 2:10

Ephesians 4:11, 12

Ephesians 4:24

Ephesians 4:32

Ephesians 5:18

Ephesians 5:21

Ephesians 5:25

Ephesians 6:4

Ephesians 6:13-15

Ephesians 6:16, 17

Ephesians 6:18

Ephesians 6:19

Philippians 1:21

Philippians 2:3, 4

Philippians 2:12, 13

Philippians 3:20, 21

Philippians 4:6, 7

Philippians 4:8, 9

Philippians 4:19

Colossians 1:18

Colossians 1:28

Colossians 3:1-4

Colossians 3:12, 13

Colossians 3:16

Colossians 3:23, 24

Colossians 4:1

Colossians 4:5, 6

1 Thessalonians 5:23

1 Timothy 2:1

2 Timothy 2:2

2 Timothy 2:15

2 Timothy 3:16, 17

Titus 2:13

Titus 3:5

Hebrews 1:1, 2

Hebrews 1:14

Hebrews 4:12

Hebrews 4:15, 16

Hebrews 11:1, 6

Hebrews 13:5

James 1:17

James 1:19, 20

James 1:22

James 4:4

James 4:7

1 Peter 1:3-5

1 Peter 1:13

1 Peter 3:1, 2

1 Peter 3:7

1 Peter 3:15

1 Peter 3:18

1 Peter 4:10

1 Peter 5:5-7

1 Peter 5:8

2 Peter 1:21

1 John 1:9

1 John 2:6

1 John 2:15, 16

1 John 3:4

1 John 4:4

1 John 4:8

1 John 5:12

1 John 5:13

1 John 5:14

Jude 6

Revelation 3:20

Revelation 20:15

Part III
Scripture Prayer Guide
A thirty-one-day pattern for devotions
and Bible reading

How to Use the Scripture Prayer Guide

A thirty-one-day pattern for devotions and Bible reading

Purpose

The purpose of the Scripture Prayer Guide is to encourage you to pray Scripture back to God. The authors have compiled prayers and vital passages of Scripture and rewritten them when necessary in the first person so that you can pray them back to the Lord.

This section guides you in a clear and systematic way through the various forms of prayer to give you a greater *breadth* and *depth* in your prayer life.

How to Use It

The Scripture Prayer Guide contains a set of biblical prayers for each day of the month. Start at Day 1 at the beginning of each month and cycle through the guide twelve times a year. Because, as Scripture, these prayers are alive and powerful, you will find that praying them on a regular basis implants biblical truth within your heart and mind and gives you a greater skill in the art of prayer. The passages you pray will always be relevant to your daily needs and circumstances.

There are eight kinds of prayer in each day that will make a distinct contribution to your prayer life. This combination will give you a "balanced diet" of prayer:

1. Prayers of Adoration

Prayers of adoration are expressions of praise and worship of the person, powers, and perfections of the Lord of all creation. Each set of prayers begins with adoration to help you center your mind and heart on God. In adoration, you honor, exalt, esteem, bless, and magnify the name of the Lord as you reflect upon His goodness, grace, holiness, mercy, love, might, power, and dominion (Rev. 4:11; 5:12, 13). In praise, you rejoice in God, align yourself in obedience to Him, and express all that you have discovered Him to be.

2. Prayers for Forgiveness

Prayers for forgiveness acknowledge how we have fallen short of the glory and character of God. The more we grasp the holiness of God, the more we recognize the destructiveness and deceitfulness of sin.

You will find that the passages chosen prepare you to examine your heart and allow the Spirit of God to bring to mind specific attitudes and actions that are contrary to the character of God. By confessing your sins, you step out of the darkness and walk in fellowship with the God of light (1 John 1:5 – 2:2).

3. Prayers for Renewal

Prayers for renewal are biblical commands or truths that you pray back to God, asking Him to make them a reality in your life. In this form of prayer, you are asking for God's grace and power for spiritual, mental, and emotional renewal. The Scriptures themselves assure us that these are specific areas that are important to the heart of God.

4. Prayers for Personal Needs

Prayers for personal needs are specific requests for yourself that you bring before the Lord. In this form of prayer, you open your heart to God and express your concerns, needs, desires, and plans. It is appropriate to ask the Lord for guidance, wisdom, and enablement, because, in doing so, you are acknowledging your dependence upon Him for all things.

Prayers for personal needs are based on a one-week cycle and are organized around a different theme for each day of the week:

Day One: Spiritual Growth
                     Sensitivity to sin
                     Greater love and commitment to the
                            Lord
Day :   Special Concerns
                 My Activities for This Day

Day Two: Need for Wisdom
                     Wisdom for living life
                     Developing an eternal perspective
                     Renewal of my mind
                 Special Concerns
                 My Activities for This Day

Day Three: Spiritual Insight
                     Understanding and insight into the
                            Word

Understanding my identity in Christ
  Who I am
  Where I came from
  Why I am here
  Where I am going
The leading of the Lord and insight
    into God's will
Special Concerns
My Activities for This Day

Day Four: Relationships with Others
  Greater love and compassion for
      others
    Loved ones
    The lost
    Those in need
  Special Concerns
  My Activities for This Day

Day Five: Faithfulness as a Steward
  With my time
  With my talents
  With my treasure
  Special Concerns
  My Activities for This Day

Day Six: The Lord's Blessing and Enablement in
      My Roles
  Family
  Ministry
    Evangelism
    Discovery, development, and use of
      spiritual gifts

        Career
        Special Concerns
        My Activities for This Day

Day Seven: Personal Concerns
          Spiritual victory
            Over the world
            Over the flesh
            Over the devil
          Continuous growth as a person
          Personal discipline
          Physical health and strength
        Special Concerns
        My Activities for This Day

After the seventh day, the cycle of petitions returns to the first day.

It is helpful to personalize these petitions by jotting down specific requests applicable to each "special concerns" section. Think about all the prayer concerns you have in each category. For example, the requests on Thursday deal with time, talent, and treasure. A special concern for you in this area might be a pressing financial obligation.

5. Prayers for Others

Prayers for others focus on the needs and well-being of other people. The order of the prayers in this plan takes you from God to self to others. Prayers of adoration focus on God; prayers for forgiveness, renewal, and personal needs focus on self; and the prayers in this section emphasize others. Knowing that your deepest needs are met in Christ, you are free to look beyond yourself to the interests of others.

Prayers for others are based on a one-week cycle and are organized around a different theme for each day of the week:

Day One: The Church and Other Ministries
             My local church
             Other churches
             Other Christian ministries
             Educational institutions
             Special concerns

Day Two: Family
             My immediate family
             My relatives
             The salvation of family members
             Special concerns

Day Three: Believers
             Personal friends
             People in ministry
             Those around the world who are
                 oppressed and in need
             Special concerns

Day Four: Evangelism
             Friends
             Neighbors
             Associates
             Special opportunities

Day Five: Government
             Revival
             Local government
             State government
             National government
             Current events and concerns

Day Six: Missions
             Local missions
             National missions
             World missions
             The fulfillment of the Great
                 Commission
             Special concerns

Day Seven: World Affairs
             The poor and hungry
             The oppressed and persecuted
             Those in authority
             Peace among nations
             Current events and concerns

After the seventh day, the cycle of intercessions
returns to the first day.

As with the prayers for personal needs, it is helpful
to personalize these prayers for others by jotting
down specific requests in each "special concerns"
section.

6. Prayers of Affirmation

Prayers of affirmation acknowledge truths that God
has revealed in His Word about the fundamental

issues of life. These include truths about God and truths about us (who we are, why we are here, and where we are going).

7. Prayers of Thanksgiving

Prayers of thanksgiving express your gratitude for who God is and for what He has done. Thanksgiving is an important ingredient in prayer because it causes you to reflect upon and remember the history of God's work in your life. This, in turn, increases your confidence in the way He will continue to work as you "understand the lovingkindnesses of the LORD" (Ps. 107:43).

8. Closing Prayers

The closing prayers are rich statements of Scripture that aptly conclude your devotional time. They consist of affirmations, benedictions, and doxologies.

Suggestions

1. Whenever possible, pray these prayers aloud or under your breath. In this way you are more actively involved in the prayers, and they become more deeply ingrained in your thinking.
2. Feel free to pause and add your own prayers and responses whenever you wish; you do not need to wait until you come to the prayer prompts.
3. It is a good idea to review a memory verse from the Memory Verse Guide at the end of your prayer time so that it will be on your mind throughout the day.
4. The Personal Prayer Pages that follow the Scripture Prayer Guide are designed to encourage

you to make your own list of people and concerns as you pray through the petition and intercession sections. You will want to revise and modify them as prayers are answered and as circumstances change. You can also use these pages to record insights you have gleaned from Scripture reading, meditation, and prayer.

Day 1

Scripture Reading: Select your Scripture reading from
the Bible Reading Guide on pages 113-40.

Prayers of Adoration

Not unto us, O LORD, not unto us,
But to Your name give glory,
Because of Your mercy,
Because of Your truth.   Ps. 115:1

It is good to give thanks to the LORD,
And to sing praises to Your name, O Most High;
To declare Your lovingkindness in the morning,
And Your faithfulness every night.   Ps. 92:1, 2

Pause here to express any thoughts of adoration.

Prayers for Forgiveness

Has the LORD as great delight in burnt offerings and
    sacrifices,
As in obeying the voice of the LORD?
Behold, to obey is better than sacrifice,
And to heed than the fat of rams.   1 Sam. 15:22

The sacrifices of God are a broken spirit;
A broken and a contrite heart—
These, O God, You will not despise.   Ps. 51:17

*Pause here to ask the Spirit of God to bring to your
mind specific sins for which you need forgiveness,
and confess them to the Lord.*

Prayers for Renewal

Lord, since I have been raised with Christ, may I seek those things which are above, where Christ is, sitting at the right hand of God. May I set my mind on things above, not on things on the earth. For I have died, and my life is hidden with Christ in You. When Christ who is my life appears, then I also will appear with Him in glory. Col. 3:1-4

May I, by Your mercies, present my body a living sacrifice, holy, acceptable to You, which is my reasonable service. And may I not be conformed to this world, but be transformed by the renewing of my mind, that I may prove what is Your good and acceptable and perfect will. Rom. 12:1, 2

Pause here for any additional prayers for renewal.

Prayers for Personal Needs

Spiritual Growth
   Sensitivity to sin
   Greater love and commitment to the Lord
Special Concerns
My Activities for This Day

Prayers for Others

The Church and Other Ministries
   My local church
   Other churches
   Other Christian ministries
   Educational institutions
   Special concerns

Prayers of Affirmation

I am persuaded that neither death nor life, nor angels
nor principalities nor powers, nor things present nor
things to come, nor height nor depth, nor any other
created thing, shall be able to separate me from the
love of God which is in Christ Jesus my Lord.

Rom. 8:38, 39

Pause here to add any personal affirmations.

Prayers of Thanksgiving

I will greatly rejoice in the LORD,
My soul shall be joyful in my God;
For He has clothed me with the garments of
    salvation,
He has covered me with the robe of righteousness,
As a bridegroom decks himself with ornaments,
And as a bride adorns herself with her jewels.

Is. 61:10

*Pause here for any personal expressions of
thanksgiving.*

Closing Prayer

Oh, satisfy us early with Your mercy,
That we may rejoice and be glad all our days!

Ps. 90:14

Memory Verse: Use the Memory Verse Guide on
    pages 141-72.

Day 2

Scripture Reading: Select your Scripture reading from the Bible Reading Guide on pages 113-40.

Prayers of Adoration

Great and marvelous are Your works,
Lord God Almighty!
Just and true are Your ways,
O King of the saints!
Who shall not fear You, O Lord, and glorify Your
    name?
For You alone are holy.
For all nations shall come and worship before You,
For Your judgments have been manifested.

Rev. 15:3, 4

Pause here to express any thoughts of adoration.

Prayers for Forgiveness

Lord, You have said:

But on this one will I look:
On him who is poor and of a contrite spirit,
And who trembles at My word.

Is. 66:2

For the LORD does not see as man sees; for man looks at the outward appearance, but the LORD looks at the heart.

1 Sam. 16:7

If we confess our sins, He is faithful and just to forgive us our sins and to cleanse us from all unrighteousness.

1 John 1:9

Pause here to ask the Spirit of God to bring to your mind specific sins for which you need forgiveness, and confess them to the Lord.

Prayers for Renewal

Your Word says:

Trust in the LORD, and do good;
Dwell in the land, and feed on His faithfulness.
Delight yourself also in the LORD,
And He shall give you the desires of your heart.
Commit your way to the LORD,
Trust also in Him,
And He shall bring it to pass.
He shall bring forth your righteousness as the
    light,
And your justice as the noonday.   Ps. 37:3-6

May I trust and delight in You. May I more and more commit my way to You.

Again Your Word says:

Come, you children, listen to me;
I will teach you the fear of the LORD.
Who is the man who desires life,
And loves many days, that he may see good?
Keep your tongue from evil,
And your lips from speaking deceit.
Depart from evil and do good;
Seek peace and pursue it.
The eyes of the LORD are on the righteous,
And His ears are open to their cry.
                 Ps. 34:11-15

Pause here for any additional prayers for renewal.

Prayers for Personal Needs

Need for Wisdom
   Wisdom for living life
   Developing an eternal perspective
   Renewal of my mind
Special Concerns
My Activities for This Day

Prayers for Others

Family
   My immediate family
   My relatives
   The salvation of family members
   Special concerns

Prayers of Affirmation

By grace I have been saved through faith, and that
not of myself; it is the gift of God, not of works, lest
anyone should boast. For I am His workmanship,
created in Christ Jesus for good works, which God
prepared beforehand that I should walk in them.

Eph. 2:8, 9

Pause here to add any personal affirmations.

Prayers of Thanksgiving

Truly my soul silently waits for God;
From Him comes my salvation.
He alone is my rock and my salvation;
He is my defense;
I shall not be greatly moved.   Ps. 62:1, 2

I will both lie down in peace, and sleep;
For You alone, O LORD, make me dwell in safety.

Ps. 4:8

*Pause here for any personal expressions of
thanksgiving.*

Closing Prayer

May the God of all grace, who called us to His
eternal glory by Christ Jesus, after we have suffered
a while, perfect, establish, strengthen, and settle us.
To Him be the glory and the dominion forever and
ever.
1 Pet. 5:10, 11

Memory Verse: Use the Memory Verse Guide on
pages 141-72.

Day 3

Scripture Reading: Select your Scripture reading from
the Bible Reading Guide on pages 113-40.

Prayers of Adoration

Oh, sing to the LORD a new song!
Sing to the LORD, all the earth.
Sing to the LORD, bless His name;
Proclaim good news of His salvation from day to day.
Declare His glory among the nations,
His wonders among all peoples.
For the LORD is great and greatly to be praised;
He is to be feared above all gods.
For all the gods of the peoples are idols,
But the LORD made the heavens.
Honor and majesty are before Him;
Strength and beauty are in His sanctuary.

Ps. 96:1-6

Pause here to express any thoughts of adoration.

Prayers for Forgiveness

But He was wounded for our transgressions,
He was bruised for our iniquities;
The chastisement for our peace was upon Him,
And by His stripes we are healed.
All we like sheep have gone astray;
We have turned, every one, to his own way;
And the LORD has laid on Him the iniquity of us all.

Is. 53:5, 6

*Pause here to ask the Spirit of God to bring to your
mind specific sins for which you need forgiveness,
and confess them to the Lord.*

Prayers for Renewal

In the words of Jesus, I pray:

Our Father in heaven,
Hallowed be Your name.
Your kingdom come,
Your will be done
On earth as it is in heaven.
Give us this day our daily bread.
And forgive us our debts,
As we forgive our debtors.
And do not lead us into temptation,
But deliver us from the evil one.
For Yours is the kingdom and the power and the glory
    forever. Amen.   Matt. 6:9-13

Pause here for any additional prayers for renewal.

Prayers for Personal Needs

Spiritual Insight
   Understanding and insight into the Word
   Understanding my identity in Christ
     Who I am
     Where I came from
     Why I am here
     Where I am going
   The leading of the Lord and insight into God's will
Special Concerns
My Activities for This Day

Prayers for Others

Believers
    Personal friends
    People in ministry
    Those around the world who are oppressed and in
      need
    Special concerns

Prayers of Affirmation

Your sheep hear Your voice, and You know them, and
they follow You. And You give them eternal life, and
they shall never perish; neither shall anyone snatch
them out of Your hand. The Father, who has given
them to You, is greater than all; and no one is able to
snatch them out of the Father's hand. You and the
Father are one.   John 10:27-30

Pause here to add any personal affirmations.

Prayers of Thanksgiving

You are my rock and my fortress and my deliverer;
The God of my strength, in whom I will trust;
My shield and the horn of my salvation,
My stronghold and my refuge;
My Savior, You save me from violence.
                                                2 Sam. 22:2, 3

*Pause here for any personal expressions of
thanksgiving.*

Closing Prayer

Now to Him who is able to keep us from stumbling,
And to present us faultless
Before the presence of His glory with exceeding joy,
To God our Savior,
Who alone is wise,
Be glory and majesty,
Dominion and power,
Both now and forever. Amen.   Jude 24, 25

Memory Verse: Use the Memory Verse Guide on
     pages 141-72.

Day 4

Scripture Reading: Select your Scripture reading from the Bible Reading Guide on pages 113-40.

Prayers of Adoration

I will extol You, my God, O King;
And I will bless Your name forever and ever.
Every day I will bless You,
And I will praise Your name forever and ever.
Great is the LORD, and greatly to be praised;
And His greatness is unsearchable.
One generation shall praise Your works to another,
And shall declare Your mighty acts.
I will meditate on the glorious splendor of Your majesty,
And on Your wondrous works.
Men shall speak of the might of Your awesome acts,
And I will declare Your greatness.
They shall utter the memory of Your great goodness,
And shall sing of Your righteousness.
The LORD is gracious and full of compassion,
Slow to anger and great in mercy.
The LORD is good to all,
And His tender mercies are over all His works.

Ps. 145:1-9

Pause here to express any thoughts of adoration.

Prayers for Forgiveness

"Now, therefore," says the LORD,
"Turn to Me with all your heart,

With fasting, with weeping, and with mourning."
So rend your heart, and not your garments;
Return to the LORD your God,
For He is gracious and merciful,
Slow to anger, and of great kindness,
And He relents from doing harm.   Joel 2:12, 13

*Pause here to ask the Spirit of God to bring to your
mind specific sins for which you need forgiveness,
and confess them to the Lord.*

Prayers for Renewal

And now, what does the LORD your God require of
you, but to fear Him, to walk in all His ways and to
love Him, to serve Him with all your heart and with
all your soul?   Deut. 10:12

This, Lord, is my prayer.

Pause here for any additional prayers for renewal.

Prayers for Personal Needs

Relationships with Others
   Greater love and compassion for others
      Loved ones
      The lost
      Those in need
Special Concerns
My Activities for This Day

Prayers for Others

Evangelism
  Friends
  Neighbors
  Associates
  Special opportunities

Prayers of Affirmation

You delivered me from the power of darkness and
conveyed me into the kingdom of the Son of Your
love, in whom I have redemption through His blood,
the forgiveness of sins.   Col. 1:13, 14

Pause here to add any personal affirmations.

Prayers of Thanksgiving

Oh, give thanks to the LORD, for He is good!
For His mercy endures forever.   1 Chr. 16:34

For who is God, except the LORD?
And who is a rock, except our God?
God is my strength and power,
And He makes my way perfect.
He makes my feet like the feet of deer,
And sets me on my high places.   2 Sam. 22:32-34

*Pause here for any personal expressions of
thanksgiving.*

Closing Prayers

This is the day the LORD has made;
We will rejoice and be glad in it.   Ps. 118:24

The grace of the Lord Jesus Christ, and the love of
God, and the communion of the Holy Spirit be with
us.   2 Cor. 13:14

Memory Verse: Use the Memory Verse Guide on
    pages 141-72.

Day 5

Scripture Reading: Select your Scripture reading from
the Bible Reading Guide on pages 113-40.

Prayers of Adoration

O LORD, our Lord,
How excellent is Your name in all the earth,
Who have set Your glory above the heavens!

Ps. 8:1

You are the Root and the Offspring of
David, the Bright and Morning Star.　　　Rev. 22:16

Blessed be the LORD God, the God of Israel,
Who only does wondrous things!
And blessed be His glorious name forever!
And let the whole earth be filled with His glory.
Amen and Amen.　　　　　　　　　Ps. 72:18, 19

Pause here to express any thoughts of adoration.

Prayers for Forgiveness

The LORD is near to those who have a broken heart,
And saves such as have a contrite spirit.

Ps. 34:18

O LORD, I have heard Your speech and was afraid.
O LORD, revive Your work in the midst of the years!
In the midst of the years make it known;
In wrath remember mercy.　　　　　　　Hab. 3:2

Thank You that You have said:

Come now, and let us reason together.
Though your sins are like scarlet,
They shall be as white as snow;
Though they are red like crimson,
They shall be as wool.   Is. 1:18

*Pause here to ask the Spirit of God to bring to your
mind specific sins for which you need forgiveness,
and confess them to the Lord.*

Prayers for Renewal

May I cast down arguments and every high thing that
exalts itself against the knowledge of You, and bring
every thought into captivity to the obedience of
Christ.   2 Cor. 10:5

May I seek first Your kingdom and Your righteousness, and may all these things be added to me.
                                                Matt. 6:33

Having found one pearl of great price, may I go and
sell all that I have, and buy it.   Matt. 13:46

Pause here for any additional prayers for renewal.

Prayers for Personal Needs

Faithfulness as a Steward
    With my time
    With my talents
    With my treasure
Special Concerns
My Activities for This Day

Prayers for Others

Government
    Revival
    Local government
    State government
    National government
    Current events and concerns

Prayers of Affirmation

You are the resurrection and the life. He who believes
in You, though he may die, he shall live. And whoever
lives and believes in You shall never die.

John 11:25, 26

Pause here to add any personal affirmations.

Prayers of Thanksgiving

Bless the LORD, O my soul;
And all that is within me, bless His holy name!
Bless the LORD, O my soul,
And forget not all His benefits:
Who forgives all your iniquities,
Who heals all your diseases,
Who redeems your life from destruction,
Who crowns you with lovingkindness and tender
    mercies,
Who satisfies your mouth with good things,
So that your youth is renewed like the eagle's.

Ps. 103:1-5

*Pause here for any personal expressions of
thanksgiving.*

Closing Prayer

Now to Him who is able to establish us according to the gospel and the preaching of Jesus Christ, to God, alone wise, be glory through Jesus Christ forever. Amen.   Rom. 16:25, 27

Memory Verse: Use the Memory Verse Guide on
   pages 141-72.

Day 6

Scripture Reading: Select your Scripture reading from
the Bible Reading Guide on pages 113-40.

Prayers of Adoration

Rejoice in the LORD, O you righteous!
For praise from the upright is beautiful.   Ps. 33:1

I will bless the LORD at all times;
His praise shall continually be in my mouth.
My soul shall make its boast in the LORD;
The humble shall hear of it and be glad.
Oh, magnify the LORD with me,
And let us exalt His name together.   Ps. 34:1-3

Pause here to express any thoughts of adoration.

Prayers for Forgiveness

Who can understand his errors?
Cleanse me from secret faults.
Keep back Your servant also from presumptuous
     sins;
Let them not have dominion over me.
Then I shall be blameless,
And I shall be innocent of great transgression.

                                        Ps. 19:12, 13

Thank You, Lord, that You have said:

For a mere moment I have forsaken you,
But with great mercies I will gather you.
With a little wrath I hid My face from you for a
     moment;

But with everlasting kindness I will have mercy on
    you.   Is. 54:7, 8

*Pause here to ask the Spirit of God to bring to your
mind specific sins for which you need forgiveness,
and confess them to the Lord.*

Prayers for Renewal

Show me Your ways, O LORD;
Teach me Your paths.
Lead me in Your truth and teach me,
For You are the God of my salvation;
On You I wait all the day.
Remember, O LORD, Your tender mercies and Your
    lovingkindnesses,
For they are from of old.   Ps. 25:4-6

LORD, make me to know my end,
And what is the measure of my days,
That I may know how frail I am.   Ps. 39:4

So teach me to number my days,
That I may gain a heart of wisdom.   Ps. 90:12

Pause here for any additional prayers for renewal.

Prayers for Personal Needs

The Lord's Blessing and Enablement in My Roles
    Family
    Ministry
        Evangelism

Discovery, development, and use of spiritual gifts
Career
Special Concerns
My Activities for This Day

Prayers for Others

Missions
    Local missions
    National missions
    World missions
    The fulfillment of the Great Commission
    Special concerns

Prayers of Affirmation

Having been justified by faith, I have peace with God through my Lord Jesus Christ, through whom also I have access by faith into this grace in which I stand, and rejoice in hope of the glory of God.

Rom. 5:1, 2

Pause here to add any personal affirmations.

Prayers of Thanksgiving

He who dwells in the secret place of the Most High
Shall abide under the shadow of the Almighty.
I will say of the LORD, "He is my refuge and my
    fortress;
My God, in Him I will trust."   Ps. 91:1, 2

Pause here for any personal expressions of thanksgiving.

Closing Prayer

Surely goodness and mercy shall follow me
All the days of my life;
And I will dwell in the house of the LORD
Forever.   Ps. 23:6

Memory Verse: Use the Memory Verse Guide on
    pages 141-72.

Day 7

Scripture Reading: Select your Scripture reading from
the Bible Reading Guide on pages 113-40.

Prayers of Adoration

But I will hope continually,
And will praise You yet more and more.
My mouth shall tell of Your righteousness
And Your salvation all the day,
For I do not know their limits.
I will go in the strength of the Lord GOD;
I will make mention of Your righteousness, of Yours
    only.
O God, You have taught me from my youth;
And to this day I declare Your wondrous works.

Ps. 71:14-17

Pause here to express any thoughts of adoration.

Prayers for Forgiveness

Have mercy upon me, O God,
According to Your lovingkindness;
According to the multitude of Your tender mercies,
Blot out my transgressions.
Wash me thoroughly from my iniquity,
And cleanse me from my sin.
For I acknowledge my transgressions,
And my sin is always before me.
Against You, You only, have I sinned,
And done this evil in Your sight—
That You may be found just when You speak,
And blameless when You judge.   Ps. 51:1-4

*Pause here to ask the Spirit of God to bring to your
mind specific sins for which you need forgiveness,
and confess them to the Lord.*

Prayers for Renewal

May these beatitudes be a reality in my life:

Blessed are the poor in spirit,
    For theirs is the kingdom of heaven.
Blessed are those who mourn,
    For they shall be comforted.
Blessed are the meek,
    For they shall inherit the earth.
Blessed are those who hunger and thirst for
    righteousness,
    For they shall be filled.
Blessed are the merciful,
    For they shall obtain mercy.
Blessed are the pure in heart,
    For they shall see God.
Blessed are the peacemakers,
    For they shall be called sons of God.
Blessed are those who are persecuted for
    righteousness' sake,
    For theirs is the kingdom of heaven.

Matt. 5:3-10

Pause here for any additional prayers for renewal.

Prayers for Personal Needs

Personal Concerns
    Spiritual victory
        Over the world
        Over the flesh

    Over the Devil
   Continuous growth as a person
   Personal discipline
   Physical health and strength
Special Concerns
My Activities for This Day

Prayers for Others

World Affairs
   The poor and hungry
   The oppressed and persecuted
   Those in authority
   Peace among nations
   Current events and concerns

Prayers of Affirmation

I may come to You, weary and heavy laden, and You
will give me rest. I may take Your yoke upon me, and
learn from You, for You are gentle and lowly in heart,
and I shall find rest for my soul. For Your yoke is
easy, and Your burden is light.   Matt. 11:28-30

Pause here to add any personal affirmations.

Prayers of Thanksgiving

He who dwells in the secret place of the Most High
Shall abide under the shadow of the Almighty.
I will say of the LORD, "He is my refuge and my
   fortress;
My God, in Him I will trust."   Ps. 91:1, 2

*Pause here for any personal expressions of
thanksgiving.*

Closing Prayer

Blessing and honor and glory and power
Be to Him who sits on the throne,
And to the Lamb, forever and forever!   Rev. 5:13

Memory Verse: Use the Memory Verse Guide on
     pages 141-72.

Day 8

Scripture Reading: Select your Scripture reading from
the Bible Reading Guide on pages 113-40.

Prayers of Adoration

Make a joyful shout to the LORD, all you lands!
Serve the LORD with gladness;
Come before His presence with singing.
Know that the LORD, He is God;
It is He who has made us, and not we ourselves;
We are His people and the sheep of His pasture.
Enter into His gates with thanksgiving,
And into His courts with praise.
Be thankful to Him, and bless His name.
For the LORD is good;
His mercy is everlasting,
And His truth endures to all generations.

Ps. 100:1-5

Pause here to express any thoughts of adoration.

Prayers for Forgiveness

Purge me with hyssop, and I shall be clean;
Wash me, and I shall be whiter than snow.
Make me hear joy and gladness,
That the bones You have broken may rejoice.
Hide Your face from my sins,
And blot out all my iniquities.
Create in me a clean heart, O God,
And renew a steadfast spirit within me.
Do not cast me away from Your presence,
And do not take Your Holy Spirit from me.

Restore to me the joy of Your salvation,
And uphold me by Your generous Spirit.
Then I will teach transgressors Your ways,
And sinners shall be converted to You.

Ps. 51:7-13

*Pause here to ask the Spirit of God to bring to your
mind specific sins for which you need forgiveness,
and confess them to the Lord.*

Prayers for Renewal

Incline my heart to Your testimonies,
And not to covetousness.
Turn away my eyes from looking at worthless things,
And revive me in Your way.   Ps. 119:36, 37

Let my conduct be without covetousness, being
content with what I have. For You Yourself have said,
"I will never leave you nor forsake you."   Heb. 13:5

Pause here for any additional prayers for renewal.

Prayers for Personal Needs

Spiritual Growth
   Sensitivity to sin
   Greater love and commitment to the Lord
Special Concerns
My Activities for This Day

Prayers for Others

The Church and Other Ministries
   My local church
   Other churches

Other Christian ministries
Educational institutions
Special concerns

Prayers of Affirmation

You are the light of the world. He who follows You shall not walk in the darkness, but have the light of life. John 8:12

You are the bread of life. He who comes to You shall never hunger, and he who believes in You shall never thirst. John 6:35

Whoever drinks of the water that You shall give him will never thirst. But the water that You shall give him will become in him a fountain of water springing up into everlasting life. John 4:14

Pause here to add any personal affirmations.

Prayers of Thanksgiving

The LORD is my light and my salvation;
Whom shall I fear?
The LORD is the strength of my life;
Of whom shall I be afraid? Ps. 27:1

But to you who fear My name
The Sun of Righteousness shall arise
With healing in His wings;
And you shall go out
And grow fat like stall-fed calves. Mal. 4:2

*Pause here for any personal expressions of
thanksgiving.*

Closing Prayer

Now may the God of peace who brought up our Lord Jesus from the dead, that great Shepherd of the sheep, through the blood of the everlasting covenant, make us complete in every good work to do His will, working in us what is well pleasing in His sight, through Jesus Christ, to whom be glory forever and ever. Amen.   Heb. 13:20, 21

Memory Verse: Use the Memory Verse Guide on
    pages 141-72.

Day 9

Scripture Reading: Select your Scripture reading from
the Bible Reading Guide on pages 113-40.

Prayers of Adoration

Oh, taste and see that the LORD is good;
Blessed is the man who trusts in Him!
Oh, fear the LORD, you His saints!
There is no want to those who fear Him.

Ps. 34:8, 9

I will praise You, for I am fearfully and wonderfully
    made;
Marvelous are Your works,
And that my soul knows very well.   Ps. 139:14

Pause here to express any thoughts of adoration.

Prayers for Forgiveness

Blessed is he whose transgression is forgiven,
Whose sin is covered.
Blessed is the man to whom the LORD does not
    impute iniquity,
And in whose spirit there is no deceit.
When I kept silent, my bones grew old
Through my groaning all the day long.
For day and night Your hand was heavy upon me;
My vitality was turned into the drought of summer.
I acknowledged my sin to You,
And my iniquity I have not hidden.

I said, "I will confess my transgressions to the
    LORD,"
And You forgave the iniquity of my sin.

Ps. 32:1-5

*Pause here to ask the Spirit of God to bring to your
mind specific sins for which you need forgiveness,
and confess them to the Lord.*

Prayers for Renewal

Concerning stewardship, Your Word says:

It is required in stewards that one be found faithful.

1 Cor. 4:2

And that:

No servant can serve two masters; for either he will
hate the one and love the other, or else he will be
loyal to the one and despise the other. You cannot
serve God and mammon.

Luke 16:13

And that:

His lord said to him, "Well done, good and faithful
servant; you were faithful over a few things, I will
make you ruler over many things. Enter into the joy
of your lord."

Matt. 25:21

May I be a faithful steward and enter into Your joy.

Pause here for any additional prayers for renewal.

Prayers for Personal Needs

Need for Wisdom
    Wisdom for living life

Developing an eternal perspective
Renewal of my mind
Special Concerns
My Activities for This Day

Prayers for Others

Family
My immediate family
My relatives
The salvation of family members
Special concerns

Prayers of Affirmation

Since I am in Christ, I am a new creation; old things
have passed away; behold, all things have become
new. 2 Cor. 5:17

I reckon myself to be dead indeed to sin, but alive to
God in Christ Jesus our Lord. Rom. 6:11

Pause here to add any personal affirmations.

Prayers of Thanksgiving

Lord, thank You that You have made this promise:

Because he has set his love upon Me, therefore I will
    deliver him;
I will set him on high, because he has known My
    name.
He shall call upon Me, and I will answer him;
I will be with him in trouble;
I will deliver him and honor him.

With long life I will satisfy him,
And show him My salvation.   Ps. 91:14-16

*Pause here for any personal expressions of
thanksgiving.*

Closing Prayer

Let the words of my mouth and the meditation of my
    heart
Be acceptable in Your sight,
O LORD, my strength and my Redeemer.

                                        Ps. 19:14

Memory Verse: Use the Memory Verse Guide on
    pages 141-72.

Day 10

Scripture Reading: Select your Scripture reading from
   the Bible Reading Guide on pages 113-40.

Prayers of Adoration

All Your works shall praise You, O LORD,
And Your saints shall bless You.
They shall speak of the glory of Your kingdom,
And talk of Your power,
To make known to the sons of men His mighty acts,
And the glorious majesty of His kingdom.
Your kingdom is an everlasting kingdom,
And Your dominion endures throughout all
   generations.   Ps. 145:10-13

Pause here to express any thoughts of adoration.

Prayers for Forgiveness

God is wise in heart and mighty in strength.
Who has hardened himself against Him and
   prospered?   Job 9:4

Come, and let us return to the LORD;
For He has torn, but He will heal us;
He has stricken, but He will bind us up.
After two days He will revive us;
On the third day He will raise us up,
That we may live in His sight.   Hos. 6:1, 2

*Pause here to ask the Spirit of God to bring to your
mind specific sins for which you need forgiveness,
and confess them to the Lord.*

Prayers for Renewal

If you abide in Me, and My words abide in you, you
will ask what you desire, and it shall be done for you.
By this My Father is glorified, that you bear much
fruit; so you will be My disciples. As the Father
loved Me, I also have loved you; abide in My love. If
you keep My commandments, you will abide in My
love, just as I have kept My Father's commandments
and abide in His love. These things I have spoken to
you, that My joy may remain in you, and that your joy
may be full.   John 15:7-11

Lord Jesus, let me abide in Your love today.

Pause here for any additional prayers for renewal.

Prayers for Personal Needs

Spiritual Insight
   Understanding and insight into the Word
   Understanding my identity in Christ
      Who I am
      Where I came from
      Why I am here
      Where I am going
   The leading of the Lord and insight into God's will
Special Concerns
My Activities for This Day

Prayers for Others

Believers
 Personal friends
 People in ministry
 Those around the world who are oppressed and in
 need
 Special concerns

Prayers of Affirmation

I have been crucified with Christ; it is no longer I
who live, but Christ lives in me; and the life which I
now live in the flesh I live by faith in the Son of God,
who loved me and gave Himself for me.   Gal. 2:20

Pause here to add any personal affirmations.

Prayers of Thanksgiving

Blessed be the God and Father of our Lord Jesus
Christ, who according to His abundant mercy has
begotten us again to a living hope through the
resurrection of Jesus Christ from the dead, to an
inheritance incorruptible and undefiled and that does
not fade away, reserved in heaven for you, who are
kept by the power of God through faith for salvation
ready to be revealed in the last time.   1 Pet. 1:3-5

*Pause here for any personal expressions of
thanksgiving.*

Closing Prayer

Now to Him who is able to do exceedingly
abundantly above all that we ask or think, according

to the power that works in us, to Him be glory in the church by Christ Jesus to all generations, forever and ever. Amen.   Eph. 3:20, 21

Memory Verse: Use the Memory Verse Guide on
    pages 141-72.

Day 11

Scripture Reading: Select your Scripture reading from
the Bible Reading Guide on pages 113-40.

Prayers of Adoration

Blessed are You, LORD God of Israel, our Father,
forever and ever.
Yours, O LORD, is the greatness,
The power and the glory,
The victory and the majesty;
For all that is in heaven and in earth is Yours;
Yours is the kingdom, O LORD,
And You are exalted as head over all.
Both riches and honor come from You,
And You reign over all.
In Your hand it is to make great
And to give strength to all.
Now therefore, our God,
We thank You
And praise Your glorious name. 1 Chr. 29:10-13

Pause here to express any thoughts of adoration.

Prayers for Forgiveness

Thank You, Lord, that You have said:

I, even I, am He who blots out your transgressions
for My own sake;
And I will not remember your sins. Is. 43:25

For thus says the Lord GOD, the Holy One of Israel:

"In returning and rest you shall be saved;

In quietness and confidence shall be your strength."

Is. 30:15

*Pause here to ask the Spirit of God to bring to your
mind specific sins for which you need forgiveness,
and confess them to the Lord.*

Prayers for Renewal

Search me, O God, and know my heart;
Try me, and know my anxieties;
And see if there is any wicked way in me,
And lead me in the way everlasting.

Ps. 139:23, 24

Set a guard, O LORD, over my mouth;
Keep watch over the door of my lips.
Do not incline my heart to any evil thing.

Ps. 141:3, 4

Direct my steps in Your word,
And let no iniquity have dominion over me.

Ps. 119:133

Pause here for any additional prayers for renewal.

Prayers for Personal Needs

Relationships with Others
   Greater love and compassion for others
      Loved ones
      The lost
      Those in need
Special Concerns
My Activities for This Day

Prayers for Others

Evangelism
  Friends
  Neighbors
  Associates
  Special opportunities

Prayers of Affirmation

For I have not received the spirit of bondage again to
fear, but I have received the Spirit of adoption by
whom I cry out, "Abba, Father." Rom. 8:15

Pause here to add any personal affirmations.

Prayers of Thanksgiving

Whom have I in heaven but You?
And there is none upon earth that I desire besides
    You.
My flesh and my heart fail;
But God is the strength of my heart and my portion
    forever. Ps. 73:25, 26

Why are you cast down, O my soul?
And why are you disquieted within me?
Hope in God;
For I shall yet praise Him,
The help of my countenance and my God.

Ps. 42:11

*Pause here for any personal expressions of
thanksgiving.*

Closing Prayer

The LORD shall preserve you from all evil;
He shall preserve your soul.
The LORD shall preserve your going out and your
    coming in
From this time forth, and even forevermore.

Ps. 121:7, 8

Memory Verse: Use the Memory Verse Guide on
    pages 141-72.

Day 12

Scripture Reading: Select your Scripture reading from
the Bible Reading Guide on pages 113-40.

Prayers of Adoration

Praise the LORD!
For it is good to sing praises to our God;
For it is pleasant, and praise is beautiful.

Ps. 147:1

Blessed be the name of God forever and ever,
For wisdom and might are His.
And He changes the times and the seasons;
He removes kings and raises up kings;
He gives wisdom to the wise
And knowledge to those who have understanding.
He reveals deep and secret things;
He knows what is in the darkness,
And light dwells with Him. Dan. 2:20-22

Pause here to express any thoughts of adoration.

Prayers for Forgiveness

O LORD, do not rebuke me in Your anger,
Nor chasten me in Your hot displeasure.
Have mercy on me, O LORD, for I am weak;
O LORD, heal me, for my bones are troubled.
My soul also is greatly troubled. Ps. 6:1-3

*Pause here to ask the Spirit of God to bring to your
mind specific sins for which you need forgiveness,
and confess them to the Lord.*

Prayers for Renewal

Giving all diligence, may I add to my faith virtue,
to virtue knowledge, to knowledge self-control, to
self-control perseverance, to perseverance godliness,
to godliness brotherly kindness, and to brotherly
kindness love. 2 Pet. 1:5-7

May I not go on presenting the members of my body
as instruments of unrighteousness to sin, but may I
present myself to You as being alive from the dead,
and my members as instruments of righteousness to
You. Rom. 6:13

Father, as a sojourner and pilgrim, grant that I may
abstain from fleshly lusts which wage war against
my soul. 1 Pet. 2:11

Pause here for any additional prayers for renewal.

Prayers for Personal Needs

Faithfulness as a Steward
   With my time
   With my talents
   With my treasure
Special Concerns
My Activities for This Day

Prayers for Others

Government
   Revival
   Local government

State government
National government
Current events and concerns

Prayers of Affirmation

My body is the temple of the Holy Spirit who is in
me, whom I have from God, and I am not my own.
For I have been bought with a price; therefore I will
glorify God in my body and in my spirit, which are
God's.   1 Cor. 6:19

Pause here to add any personal affirmations.

Prayers of Thanksgiving

Through the LORD's mercies we are not consumed,
Because His compassions fail not.
They are new every morning;
Great is Your faithfulness.   Lam. 3:22, 23

*Pause here for any personal expressions of
thanksgiving.*

Closing Prayer

The LORD bless you and keep you;
The LORD make His face shine upon you,
And be gracious to you;
The LORD lift up His countenance upon you,
And give you peace.   Num. 6:24-26

Memory Verse: Use the Memory Verse Guide on
      pages 141-72.

Day 13

Scripture Reading: Select your Scripture reading from
the Bible Reading Guide on pages 113-40.

Prayers of Adoration

O God, You are my God;
Early will I seek You;
My soul thirsts for You;
My flesh longs for You
In a dry and thirsty land
Where there is no water.
So I have looked for You in the sanctuary,
To see Your power and Your glory.
Because Your lovingkindness is better than life,
My lips shall praise You.
Thus I will bless You while I live;
I will lift up my hands in Your name.
My soul shall be satisfied as with marrow and
    fatness,
And my mouth shall praise You with joyful lips.
When I remember You on my bed,
I meditate on You in the night watches,
Because You have been my help,
Therefore in the shadow of Your wings I will rejoice.

Ps. 63:1-7

The LORD lives!
Blessed be my Rock!
Let God be exalted,
The Rock of my salvation! 2 Sam. 22:47

Pause here to express any thoughts of adoration.

Prayers for Forgiveness

LORD, be merciful to me;
Heal my soul, for I have sinned against You.

Ps. 41:4

Heal me, O LORD, and I shall be healed;
Save me, and I shall be saved,
For You are my praise.

Jer. 17:14

*Pause here to ask the Spirit of God to bring to your
mind specific sins for which you need forgiveness,
and confess them to the Lord.*

Prayers for Renewal

Concerning love, You have said:

You shall love the LORD your God with all your heart,
with all your soul, and with all your mind.

Matt. 22:37

You shall love your neighbor as yourself.

Matt. 22:39

Therefore, whatever you want men to do to you, do
also to them, for this is the Law and the Prophets.

Matt. 7:12

Pause here for any additional prayers for renewal.

Prayers for Personal Needs

The Lord's Blessing and Enablement in My Roles
    Family
    Ministry
      Evangelism

   Discovery, development, and use of spiritual gifts
   Career
Special Concerns
My Activities for This Day

Prayers for Others

Missions
   Local missions
   National missions
   World missions
   The fulfillment of the Great Commission
   Special concerns

Prayers of Affirmation

You have shown us what is good;
And what do You require of us
But to do justly,
To love mercy,
And to walk humbly with You?   Mic. 6:8

Pause here to add any personal affirmations.

Prayers of Thanksgiving

God is our refuge and strength,
A very present help in trouble.   Ps. 46:1

Therefore by Him let us continually offer the sacrifice
of praise to God, that is, the fruit of our lips, giving
thanks to His name.   Heb. 13:15

*Pause here for any personal expressions of
thanksgiving.*

Closing Prayer

Now may the God of hope fill us with all joy and peace in believing, that we may abound in hope by the power of the Holy Spirit. Rom. 15:13

Memory Verse: Use the Memory Verse Guide on pages 141-72.

Day 14

Scripture Reading: Select your Scripture reading from
the Bible Reading Guide on pages 113-40.

Prayers of Adoration

Give to the LORD, O families of the peoples,
Give to the LORD glory and strength.
Give to the LORD the glory due His name;
Bring an offering, and come before Him.
Oh, worship the LORD in the beauty of holiness!
Tremble before Him, all the earth.

1 Chr. 16:28-30

For with You is the fountain of life;
In Your light we see light.　　　　　Ps. 36:9

Pause here to express any thoughts of adoration.

Prayers for Forgiveness

Woe is me, for I am undone!
Because I am a man of unclean lips.　　　　Is. 6:5

For there is not a just man on earth who does good
And does not sin.　　　　　Eccl. 7:20

Indeed I have sinned against the LORD God of Israel.

Josh. 7:20

If we say that we have no sin, we deceive ourselves,
and the truth is not in us. If we confess our sins, He
is faithful and just to forgive us our sins and to
cleanse us from all unrighteousness.　　1 John 1:8, 9

Pause here to ask the Spirit of God to bring to your mind specific sins for which you need forgiveness, and confess them to the Lord.

Prayers for Renewal

Love suffers long and is kind; love does not envy; love does not parade itself, is not puffed up; does not behave rudely, does not seek its own, is not provoked, thinks no evil; does not rejoice in iniquity, but rejoices in the truth; bears all things, believes all things, hopes all things, endures all things. Love never fails.   1 Cor. 13:4-8

Pause here for any additional prayers for renewal.

Prayers for Personal Needs

Personal Concerns
   Spiritual victory
      Over the world
      Over the flesh
      Over the Devil
   Continuous growth as a person
   Personal discipline
   Physical health and strength
Special Concerns
My Activities for This Day

Prayers for Others

World Affairs
   The poor and hungry
   The oppressed and persecuted
   Those in authority

Peace among nations
Current events and concerns

Prayers of Affirmation

For the weapons of our warfare are not carnal but
mighty in God for pulling down strongholds, casting
down arguments and every high thing that exalts
itself against the knowledge of God, bringing every
thought into captivity to the obedience of Christ.

2 Cor. 10:4, 5

Pause here to add any personal affirmations.

Prayers of Thanksgiving

My heart rejoices in the LORD;
My horn is exalted in the LORD.
No one is holy like the LORD,
For there is none besides You,
Nor is there any rock like our God.   1 Sam. 2:1, 2

*Pause here for any personal expressions of
thanksgiving.*

Closing Prayer

So teach us to number our days,
That we may gain a heart of wisdom.   Ps. 90:12

Memory Verse: Use the Memory Verse Guide on
pages 141-72.

Day 15

Scripture Reading: Select your Scripture reading from
the Bible Reading Guide on pages 113-40.

Prayers of Adoration

Oh come, let us sing to the LORD!
Let us shout joyfully to the Rock of our salvation.
Let us come before His presence with thanksgiving;
Let us shout joyfully to Him with psalms.
For the LORD is the great God,
And the great King above all gods.
Oh come, let us worship and bow down;
Let us kneel before the LORD our Maker.
For He is our God,
And we are the people of His pasture,
And the sheep of His hand.   Ps. 95:1-3, 6, 7

Pause here to express any thoughts of adoration.

Prayers for Forgiveness

Sing praise to the LORD, you saints of His,
And give thanks at the remembrance of His holy
     name.
For His anger is but for a moment,
His favor is for life;
Weeping may endure for a night,
But joy comes in the morning.   Ps. 30:4, 5

*Pause here to ask the Spirit of God to bring to your
mind specific sins for which you need forgiveness,
and confess them to the Lord.*

Prayers for Renewal

May no corrupt word proceed out of my mouth, but what is good for necessary edification, that it may impart grace to the hearers. May I not grieve the Holy Spirit of God, by whom I was sealed for the day of redemption. May all bitterness, wrath, anger, clamor, and evil speaking be put away from me, with all malice. And may I be kind to others, tender-hearted, forgiving others, even as God in Christ forgave me. Eph. 4:29-32

Pause here for any additional prayers for renewal.

Prayers for Personal Needs

Spiritual Growth
   Sensitivity to sin
   Greater love and commitment to the Lord
Special Concerns
My Activities for This Day

Prayers for Others

The Church and Other Ministries
   My local church
   Other churches
   Other Christian ministries
   Educational institutions
   Special concerns

Prayers of Affirmation

All that is in the world—the lust of the flesh, the lust of the eyes, and the pride of life—is not of the Father but is of the world. And the world is passing away,

and the lust of it; but he who does the will of God
abides forever. 1 John 2:16, 17

Pause here to add any personal affirmations.

Prayers of Thanksgiving

Sing to the LORD, all the earth;
Proclaim the good news of His salvation from day to
   day.
Declare His glory among the nations,
His wonders among all peoples.
For the LORD is great and greatly to be praised;
He is also to be feared above all gods.
For all the gods of the peoples are idols,
But the LORD made the heavens.
Honor and majesty are before Him;
Strength and gladness are in His place.
1 Chr. 16:23-27

*Pause here for any personal expressions of
thanksgiving.*

Closing Prayer

Now to the King eternal, immortal, invisible, to God
who alone is wise, be honor and glory forever and
ever. Amen. 1 Tim. 1:17

Memory Verse: Use the Memory Verse Guide on
   pages 141-72.

Day 16

Scripture Reading: Select your Scripture reading from
the Bible Reading Guide on pages 113-40.

Prayers of Adoration

I will sing to the LORD as long as I live;
I will sing praise to my God while I have my being.
May my meditation be sweet to Him;
I will be glad in the LORD.   Ps. 104:33, 34

Make a joyful shout to God, all the earth!
Sing out the honor of His name;
Make His praise glorious.
Say to God,
"How awesome are Your works!
All the earth shall worship You
And sing praises to You;
They shall sing praises to Your name."   Ps. 66:1-4

Pause here to express any thoughts of adoration.

Prayers for Forgiveness

Out of the depths I have cried to You, O LORD;
Lord, hear my voice!
Let Your ears be attentive
To the voice of my supplications.
If You, LORD, should mark iniquities,
O Lord, who could stand?
But there is forgiveness with You,
That You may be feared.   Ps. 130:1-4

*Pause here to ask the Spirit of God to bring to your
mind specific sins for which you need forgiveness,
and confess them to the Lord.*

Prayers for Renewal

May I do nothing from selfish ambition or conceit,
but in lowliness of mind let me esteem others better
than myself, not merely looking out for my own
interests, but also for the interests of others.

Phil. 2:3, 4

May I be of one mind with others, compassionate,
loving as a brother, tenderhearted, courteous, not
returning evil for evil or reviling for reviling, but on
the contrary blessing, knowing that I was called to
this, that I may inherit a blessing.   1 Pet. 3:8, 9

Pause here for any additional prayers for renewal.

Prayers for Personal Needs

Need for Wisdom
   Wisdom for living life
   Developing an eternal perspective
   Renewal of my mind
Special Concerns
My Activities for This Day

Prayers for Others

Family
   My immediate family
   My relatives
   The salvation of family members
   Special concerns

Prayers of Affirmation

I shall not lay up for myself treasures on earth,
where moth and rust destroy and where thieves break
in and steal; but I shall lay up for myself treasures in
heaven, where neither moth nor rust destroys and
where thieves do not break in and steal.

Matt. 6:19, 20

Pause here to add any personal affirmations.

Prayers of Thanksgiving

I will praise You, O LORD, with all my heart;
I will tell of all Your marvelous works.
I will be glad and rejoice in You;
I will sing praise to Your name, O Most High.

Ps. 9:1, 2

*Pause here for any personal expressions of
thanksgiving.*

Closing Prayer

For a day in Your courts is better than a thousand.
I would rather be a doorkeeper in the house of my
    God
Than dwell in the tents of wickedness.
For the LORD God is a sun and shield;
The LORD will give grace and glory;
No good thing will He withhold
From those who walk uprightly.
O LORD of hosts,
Blessed is the man who trusts in You!   Ps. 84:10-12

Memory Verse: Use the Memory Verse Guide on
    pages 141-72.

Day 17

Scripture Reading: Select your Scripture reading from
the Bible Reading Guide on pages 113-40.

Prayers of Adoration

Bless the LORD, O my soul!
O LORD my God, You are very great:
You are clothed with honor and majesty,
Who cover Yourself with light as with a garment,
Who stretch out the heavens like a curtain.

Ps. 104:1, 2

Pause here to express any thoughts of adoration.

Prayers for Forgiveness

You are merciful and gracious,
Slow to anger, and abounding in mercy.
You will not always strive with us,
Nor will You keep Your anger forever.
You have not dealt with us according to our sins.
Nor punished us according to our iniquities.
For as the heavens are high above the earth,
So great is Your mercy toward those who fear You;
As far as the east is from the west,
So far have You removed our transgressions from us.
As a father pities his children,
So You pity those who fear You.
For You know our frame;
You remember that we are dust.   Ps. 103:8-14

Pause here to ask the Spirit of God to bring to your mind specific sins for which you need forgiveness, and confess them to the Lord.

Prayers for Renewal

May the God of our Lord Jesus Christ, the Father of glory, give me the spirit of wisdom and revelation in the knowledge of Him. I pray that the eyes of my understanding may be enlightened; that I may know what is the hope of His calling, what are the riches of the glory of His inheritance in the saints, and what is the exceeding greatness of His power toward us who believe, according to the working of His mighty power which He worked in Christ when He raised Him from the dead and seated Him at His right hand in the heavenly places, far above all principality and power and might and dominion, and every name that is named, not only in this age, but also in that which is to come.   Eph. 1:17-21

Pause here for any additional prayers for renewal.

Prayers for Personal Needs

Spiritual Insight
   Understanding and insight into the Word
   Understanding my identity in Christ
      Who I am
      Where I came from
      Why I am here
      Where I am going
   The leading of the Lord and insight into God's will
Special Concerns
My Activities for This Day

Prayers for Others

Believers
  Personal friends
  People in ministry
  Those around the world who are oppressed and in
    need
  Special concerns

Prayers of Affirmation

I have it as my aim, whether present or absent, to be
well pleasing to Him. For we must all appear before
the judgment seat of Christ, that each one may
receive the things done in the body, according to
what he has done, whether good or bad.

2 Cor. 5:9, 10

Pause here to add any personal affirmations.

Prayers of Thanksgiving

We give You thanks, O Lord God Almighty,
The One who is and who was and who is to come,
Because You have taken Your great power and
  reigned. Rev. 11:17

*Pause here for any personal expressions of
thanksgiving.*

Closing Prayer

Blessing and glory and wisdom,
Thanksgiving and honor and power and might,
Be to our God forever and ever. Rev. 7:12

Memory Verse: Use the Memory Verse Guide on
  pages 141-72.

Day 18

Scripture Reading: Select your Scripture reading from
the Bible Reading Guide on pages 113-40.

Prayers of Adoration

The LORD is righteous in all His ways,
Gracious in all His works.
The LORD is near to all who call upon Him,
To all who call upon Him in truth.
He will fulfill the desire of those who fear Him;
He also will hear their cry and save them.
My mouth shall speak the praise of the LORD,
And all flesh shall bless His holy name
Forever and ever.   Ps. 145:17-19, 21

Pause here to express any thoughts of adoration.

Prayers for Forgiveness

You are just in all that has befallen us;
For You have dealt faithfully,
But we have done wickedly.   Neh. 9:33

I return to the LORD my God,
For I have stumbled because of my iniquity.
I take words with me,
And return to the LORD.
I say to Him,
"Take away all iniquity;
Receive me graciously,
For I will offer the sacrifices of my lips."

                                        Hos. 14:1, 2

Pause here to ask the Spirit of God to bring to your mind specific sins for which you need forgiveness, and confess them to the Lord.

Prayers for Renewal

May I rejoice always, pray without ceasing, in everything give thanks; for this is the will of God in Christ Jesus for me. May I not quench the Spirit or despise prophecies, but test all things; hold fast to what is good. May I abstain from every form of evil.

1 Thess. 5:16-22

May I count it all joy when I fall into various trials, knowing that the testing of my faith produces patience. And let patience have its perfect work, that I may be perfect and complete, lacking nothing. Grant that if I lack wisdom, I may ask of You, who give to all liberally and without reproach, and it will be given to me.

James 1:2-5

Pause here for any additional prayers for renewal.

Prayers for Personal Needs

Relationships with Others
Greater love and compassion for others
Loved ones
The lost
Those in need
Special Concerns
My Activities for This Day

Prayers for Others

Evangelism
    Friends
    Neighbors
    Associates
    Special opportunities

Prayers of Affirmation

All Scripture is given by inspiration of God, and is
profitable for doctrine, for reproof, for correction, for
instruction in righteousness, that the man of God
may be complete, thoroughly equipped for every good
work.   2 Tim. 3:16, 17

Pause here to add any personal affirmations.

Prayers of Thanksgiving

But I will sing of Your power;
Yes, I will sing aloud of Your mercy in the morning;
For You have been my defense
And refuge in the day of my trouble.
To You O my Strength, I will sing praises;
For God is my defense,
My God of mercy.   Ps. 59:16, 17

*Pause here for any personal expressions of
thanksgiving.*

Closing Prayer

Now may our Lord Jesus Christ Himself, and our
God and Father, who has loved us and given us

everlasting consolation and good hope by grace,
comfort our hearts and establish us in every good
word and work.   2 Thess. 2:16, 17

Memory Verse: Use the Memory Verse Guide on
    pages 141-72.

Day 19

Scripture Reading: Select your Scripture reading from
   the Bible Reading Guide on pages 113-40.

Prayers of Adoration

Blessed be Your glorious name,
Which is exalted above all blessing and praise!
You alone are the LORD;
You have made heaven,
The heaven of heavens, with all their host,
The earth and everything on it,
The seas and all that is in them,
And You preserve them all.
The host of heaven worships You.   Neh. 9:5, 6

Pause here to express any thoughts of adoration.

Prayers for Forgiveness

Remember, O LORD, Your tender mercies and Your
   lovingkindnesses,
For they are from of old.
Do not remember the sins of my youth, nor my
   transgressions;
According to Your mercy remember me,
For Your goodness' sake, O LORD.
Good and upright is the LORD;
Therefore He teaches sinners in the way.
The humble He guides in justice,
And the humble He teaches His way.
All the paths of the LORD are mercy and truth,
To such as keep His covenant and His testimonies.
For Your name's sake, O LORD,

Pardon my iniquity, for it is great.   Ps. 25:6-11

Pause here to ask the Spirit of God to bring to your mind specific sins for which you need forgiveness, and confess them to the Lord.

Prayers for Renewal

I pray that I may be steadfast, immovable, always abounding in the work of the Lord, knowing that my labor is not in vain in the Lord.   1 Cor. 15:58

May I be strong in the Lord and in the power of His might as I put on the whole armor of God, that I may be able to stand against the wiles of the devil.
     Eph. 6:10, 11

Pause here for any additional prayers for renewal.

Prayers for Personal Needs

Faithfulness as a Steward
     With my time
     With my talents
     With my treasure
Special Concerns
My Activities for This Day

Prayers for Others

Government
     Revival
     Local government
     State government
     National government
     Current events and concerns

Prayers of Affirmation

The word of God is living and powerful, and sharper than any two-edged sword, piercing even to the division of soul and spirit, and of joints and marrow, and is a discerner of the thoughts and intents of the heart. And there is no creature hidden from His sight, but all things are naked and open to the eyes of Him to whom we must give account.

Heb. 4:12, 13

Pause here to add any personal affirmations.

Prayers of Thanksgiving

I will sing of the mercies of the LORD forever;
With my mouth will I make known Your faithfulness
 to all generations.
For I have said, "Mercy shall be built up forever;
Your faithfulness You shall establish in the very
 heavens."

Ps. 89:1, 2

Pause here for any personal expressions of thanksgiving.

Closing Prayer

Finally, brethren, farewell. Become complete. Be of good comfort, be of one mind, live in peace; and the God of love and peace will be with you. The grace of the Lord Jesus Christ, and the love of God, and the communion of the Holy Spirit, be with you all.

2 Cor. 13:11, 14

Memory Verse: Use the Memory Verse Guide on
 pages 141-72.

Day 20

Scripture Reading: Select your Scripture reading from
the Bible Reading Guide on pages 113-40.

Prayers of Adoration

I will praise You, O Lord, among the peoples;
I will sing to You among the nations.
For Your mercy reaches unto the heavens,
And Your truth unto the clouds.
Be exalted, O God, above the heavens;
Let Your glory be above all the earth.

Ps. 57:9-11

May the glory of the LORD endure forever;
May the LORD rejoice in His works.   Ps. 104:31

Pause here to express any thoughts of adoration.

Prayers for Forgiveness

Thank You, Lord, that You have said:
I will cleanse them from all their iniquity by which
they have sinned against Me, and I will pardon all
their iniquities by which they have sinned and by
which they have transgressed against Me.

Jer. 33:8

Search me, O God, and know my heart;
Try me, and know my anxieties;
And see if there is any wicked way in me,
And lead me in the way everlasting.

Ps. 139:23, 24

*Pause here to ask the Spirit of God to bring to your
mind specific sins for which you need forgiveness,
and confess them to the Lord.*

Prayers for Renewal

Grant that I may gird up the loins of my mind, be
sober, and rest my hope fully upon the grace that is
to be brought to me at the revelation of Jesus Christ;
as an obedient child, may I not be conformed to the
former lusts, as in my ignorance; but as He who
called me is holy, may I also be holy in all my
conduct, because it is written, "Be holy, for I am
holy."   1 Pet. 1:13-16

May I be anxious for nothing, but in everything by
prayer and supplication, with thanksgiving, may I
make my requests be made known to You; and Your
peace, which surpasses all understanding, will guard
my heart and mind through Christ Jesus.

                                                       Phil. 4:6, 7

Pause here for any additional prayers for renewal.

Prayers for Personal Needs

The Lord's Blessing and Enablement in My Roles
    Family
    Ministry
        Evangelism
        Discovery, development, and use of spiritual gifts
    Career
Special Concerns
My Activities for This Day

Prayers for Others

Missions
    Local missions
    National missions
    The fulfillment of the Great Commission
    Special concerns

Prayers of Affirmation

Your word is a lamp to my feet
And a light to my path.

                              Ps. 119:105

I prepare my heart to seek the Law of the LORD, and
to do it, and to teach statutes and ordinances.

                              Ezra 7:10

I delight to do Your will, O my God,
And Your law is within my heart.

                              Ps. 40:8

Pause here to add any personal affirmations.

Prayers of Thanksgiving

Mercy and truth have met together;
Righteousness and peace have kissed.
Truth shall spring out of the earth,
And righteousness shall look down from heaven.

                              Ps. 85:10, 11

*Pause here for any personal expressions of
thanksgiving.*

Closing Prayer

He who is the blessed and only Potentate, the King of kings and Lord of lords, who alone has immortality, dwelling in unapproachable light, whom no man has seen or can see, to whom be honor and everlasting power. Amen.   1 Tim. 6:15, 16

Memory Verse: Use the Memory Verse Guide on pages 141-72.

Day 21

Scripture Reading: Select your Scripture reading from
the Bible Reading Guide on pages 113-40.

Prayers of Adoration

Praise the LORD!
Praise God in His sanctuary;
Praise Him in His mighty firmament!
Praise Him for His mighty acts;
Praise Him according to His excellent greatness!
Praise Him with the sound of the trumpet;
Praise Him with the lute and harp!
Praise Him with the timbrel and dance;
Praise Him with stringed instruments and flutes!
Praise Him with loud cymbals;
Praise Him with clashing cymbals!
Let everything that has breath praise the LORD.
Praise the LORD! Ps. 150:1-6

Pause here to express any thoughts of adoration.

Prayers for Forgiveness

O God, You know my foolishness;
And my sins are not hidden from You.
Let not those who wait for You, O Lord GOD of
    hosts, be ashamed because of me;
Let not those who seek You be confounded because
    of me, O God of Israel. Ps. 69:5, 6

*Pause here to ask the Spirit of God to bring to your
mind specific sins for which you need forgiveness,
and confess them to the Lord.*

Prayers for Renewal

Whatever things are true, whatever things are
noble, whatever things are just, whatever things are
pure, whatever things are lovely, whatever things are
of good report, if there is any virtue and if there is
anything praiseworthy — may I meditate on these
things.   Phil. 4:8

Now therefore, I pray, if I have found grace in Your
sight, show me now Your way, that I may know You
and that I may find grace in Your sight.   Ex. 33:13

Whether I eat or drink, or whatever I do, may I do all
to the glory of God.   1 Cor. 10:31

Pause here for any additional prayers for renewal.

Prayers for Personal Needs

Personal Concerns
    Spiritual victory
        Over the world
        Over the flesh
        Over the Devil
    Continuous growth as a person
    Personal discipline
    Physical health and strength
Special Concerns
My Activities for This Day

Prayers for Others

World Affairs
    The poor and hungry

The oppressed and persecuted
Those in authority
Peace among nations
Current events and concerns

Prayers of Affirmation

Therefore I do not lose heart. Even though my outward man is perishing, yet my inward man is being renewed day by day. For our light affliction, which is but for a moment, is working for me a far more exceeding and eternal weight of glory, while I look not at the things which are seen, but at the things which are not seen. For the things which are seen are temporary, but the things which are not seen are eternal. 2 Cor. 4:16-18

Pause here to add any personal affirmations.

Prayers of Thanksgiving

I will look to the LORD;
I will wait for the God of my salvation;
My God will hear me. Mic. 7:7

Blessed be the LORD,
Because He has heard the voice of my supplications!
The LORD is my strength and my shield;
My heart trusted in Him, and I am helped;
Therefore my heart greatly rejoices,
And with my song I will praise Him. Ps. 28:6, 7

Pause here for any personal expressions of thanksgiving.

Closing Prayer

Bless the LORD, all you His hosts,
You ministers of His, who do His pleasure.
Bless the LORD, all His works,
In all places of His dominion.
Bless the LORD, O my soul!   Ps. 103:21, 22

Memory Verse: Use the Memory Verse Guide on
    pages 141-72.

Day 22

Scripture Reading: Select your Scripture reading from the Bible Reading Guide on pages 113-40.

Prayers of Adoration

I will love You, O LORD, my strength.
The LORD is my rock and my fortress and my
    deliverer;
My God, my strength, in whom I will trust;
My shield and the horn of my salvation, my
    stronghold.
I will call upon the LORD, who is worthy to be
    praised;
So shall I be saved from my enemies.   Ps. 18:1-3

Pause here to express any thoughts of adoration.

Prayers for Forgiveness

Who among you fears the LORD?
Who obeys the voice of His Servant?
Who walks in darkness
And has no light?
Let him trust in the name of the LORD
And rely upon his God.   Is. 50:10

I have blotted out, like a thick cloud, your
    transgressions,
And like a cloud, your sins.
Return to Me, for I have redeemed you.   Is. 44:22

Pause here to ask the Spirit of God to bring to your mind specific sins for which you need forgiveness, and confess them to the Lord.

Prayers for Renewal

You have said:

This Book of the Law shall not depart from your mouth, but you shall meditate in it day and night, that you may observe to do according to all that is written in it. For then you will make your way prosperous, and then you will have good success.

Josh. 1:8

Grant that I may do according to all that is written in
   Your Word.

I will meditate on Your precepts,
And contemplate Your ways.
I will delight myself in Your statutes;
I will not forget Your word.
Deal bountifully with Your servant,
That I may live and keep Your word.
Open my eyes, that I may see
Wondrous things from Your law.   Ps. 119:15-18

Pause here for any additional prayers for renewal.

Prayers for Personal Needs

Spiritual Growth
   Sensitivity to sin
   Greater love and commitment to the Lord
Special Concerns
My Activities for This Day

Prayers for Others

The Church and Other Ministries
   My local church
   Other churches
   Other Christian ministries
   Educational institutions
   Special concerns

Prayers of Affirmation

Have you not known?
Have you not heard?
The everlasting God, the LORD,
The Creator of the ends of the earth,
Neither faints nor is weary.
His understanding is unsearchable.
He gives power to the weak,
And to those who have no might He increases
   strength.
Even the youths shall faint and be weary,
And the young men shall utterly fall,
But those who wait on the LORD
Shall renew their strength;
They shall mount up with wings like eagles,
They shall run and not be weary,
They shall walk and not faint.   Is. 40:28-31

Pause here to add any personal affirmations.

Prayers of Thanksgiving

The works of the LORD are great,
Studied by all who have pleasure in them.
His work is honorable and glorious,

And His righteousness endures forever.
He has made His wonderful works to be
    remembered;
The LORD is gracious and full of compassion.

Ps. 111:2-4

Oh, give thanks to the God of heaven!
For His mercy endures forever.   Ps. 136:26

*Pause here for any personal expressions of
thanksgiving.*

Closing Prayer

Grow in the grace and knowledge of our Lord and
Savior Jesus Christ. To Him be the glory both now
and forever. Amen.   2 Pet. 3:18

Memory Verse: Use the Memory Verse Guide on
    pages 141-72.

Day 23

Scripture Reading: Select your Scripture reading from the Bible Reading Guide on pages 113-40.

Prayers of Adoration

The LORD reigns,
He is clothed with majesty;
The LORD is clothed,
He has girded Himself with strength.
Surely the world is established, so that it cannot be
  moved.
Your throne is established from of old;
You are from everlasting.   Ps. 93:1, 2

Oh, the depth of the riches both of the wisdom and
knowledge of God! How unsearchable are His
judgments and His ways past finding out!
                                           Rom. 11:33

Pause here to express any thoughts of adoration.

Prayers for Forgiveness

My Son, do not despise the chastening of the LORD,
Nor be discouraged when you are rebuked by Him;
For whom the LORD loves He chastens,
And scourges every son whom He receives.

Now no chastening seems to be joyful for the
present, but painful; nevertheless, afterward it yields
the peaceable fruit of righteousness to those who
have been trained by it. Therefore strengthen the

hands which hang down, and the feeble knees, and
make straight paths for your feet, so that what is
lame may not be dislocated, but rather be healed.

Heb. 12:5, 6, 11-13

*Pause here to ask the Spirit of God to bring to your
mind specific sins for which you need forgiveness,
and confess them to the Lord.*

Prayers for Renewal

May I keep heart with all diligence,
For out of it spring the issues of life.
May I put away a deceitful mouth,
And put perverse lips far from me.
Let my eyes look straight ahead,
And my eyelids look right before me.
May I ponder the path of my feet,
And all my ways will be established.
May I not turn to the right or the left;
But remove my foot from evil.   Prov. 4:23-27

Pause here for any additional prayers for renewal.

Prayers for Personal Needs

Need for Wisdom
   Wisdom for living life
   Developing an eternal perspective
   Renewal of my mind
Special Concerns
My Activities for This Day

Prayers for Others

Family
   My immediate family
   My relatives
   The salvation of family members
   Special concerns

Prayers of Affirmation

For I consider that the sufferings of this present time
are not worthy to be compared with the glory which
shall be revealed in me.   Rom. 8:18

Pause here to add any personal affirmations.

Prayers of Thanksgiving

O Lord GOD, You have begun to show Your servant
Your greatness and Your mighty hand, for what god is
there in heaven or on earth who can do anything like
Your works and Your mighty deeds?   Deut. 3:24

I have trusted in Your mercy;
My heart shall rejoice in Your salvation.
I will sing to the LORD,
Because He has dealt bountifully with me.
                        Ps. 13:5, 6

Pause here for any personal expressions of
thanksgiving.

Closing Prayer

I would have lost heart, unless I had believed
That I would see the goodness of the LORD
In the land of the living.
Wait on the LORD;
Be of good courage,
And He shall strengthen your heart;
Wait, I say, on the LORD!   Ps. 27:13, 14

Memory Verse: Use the Memory Verse Guide on
    pages 141-72.

Day 24

Scripture Reading: Select your Scripture reading from
the Bible Reading Guide on pages 113-40.

Prayers of Adoration

Praise the LORD!
Praise, O servants of the LORD,
Praise the name of the LORD!
Blessed be the name of the LORD
From this time forth and forevermore!
From the rising of the sun to its going down
The LORD's name is to be praised.
The LORD is high above all nations,
His glory above the heavens.
Who is like the LORD our God,
Who dwells on high,
Who humbles Himself to behold
The things that are in the heavens and in the earth?

Ps. 113:1-6

Pause here to express any thoughts of adoration.

Prayers for Forgiveness

Deliver me from the guilt of bloodshed, O God,
The God of my salvation,
And my tongue shall sing aloud of Your
    righteousness.
O Lord, open my lips,
And my mouth shall show forth Your praise.
For You do not desire sacrifice, or else I would
    give it;

You do not delight in burnt offering.
The sacrifices of God are a broken spirit;
A broken and a contrite heart—
These, O God, You will not despise.

Ps. 51:14-17

*Pause here to ask the Spirit of God to bring to your
mind specific sins for which you need forgiveness,
and confess them to the Lord.*

Prayers for Renewal

May my light so shine before men that they may see
my good works and glorify my Father in heaven.

Matt. 5:16

May I do all things without complaining and
disputing, that I may become blameless and harmless, a child of God without fault in the midst of a
crooked and perverse generation, among whom I
shine as a light in the world, holding fast the word of
life.

Phil. 2:14-16

Pause here for any additional prayers for renewal.

Prayers for Personal Needs

Spiritual Insight
   Understanding and insight into the Word
   Understanding my identity in Christ
      Who I am
      Where I came from
      Why I am here
      Where I am going

The leading of the Lord and insight into God's will
Special Concerns
My Activities for This Day

Prayers for Others

Believers
    Personal friends
    People in ministry
    Those around the world who are oppressed and in
      need
    Special concerns

Prayers of Affirmation

I am always confident, knowing that while I am at
home in the body I am absent from the Lord. For I
walk by faith, not by sight. I am confident, yes, well
pleased rather to be absent from the body and to be
present with the Lord.   2 Cor. 5:6-8

Pause here to add any personal affirmations.

Prayers of Thanksgiving

Our soul waits for the LORD;
He is our help and our shield.
For our heart shall rejoice in Him,
Because we have trusted in His holy name.
Let Your mercy, O LORD, be upon us,
Just as we hope in You.   Ps. 33:20-22

Now thanks be to God who always leads us in
triumph in Christ, and through us diffuses the
fragrance of His knowledge in every place.
                                        2 Cor. 2:14

*Pause here for any personal expressions of
thanksgiving.*

Closing Prayers

Great is our Lord, and mighty in power;
His understanding is infinite.
The LORD lifts up the humble;
He casts the wicked down to the ground.

Ps. 147:5, 6

The LORD will command His lovingkindness in the
    daytime,
And in the night His song shall be with me—
A prayer to the God of my life.   Ps. 42:8

Memory Verse: Use the Memory Verse Guide on
    pages 141-72.

Day 25

Scripture Reading: Select your Scripture reading from
the Bible Reading Guide on pages 113-40.

Prayers of Adoration

I will praise You, O LORD, with my whole heart;
I will tell of all Your marvelous works.
I will be glad and rejoice in You;
I will sing praise to Your name, O Most High.

Ps. 9:1, 2

You are worthy, O Lord,
To receive glory and honor and power;
For You created all things,
And by Your will they exist and were created.

Rev. 4:11

Holy, holy, holy is the LORD of hosts;
The whole earth is full of His glory!   Is. 6:3

Let my mouth be filled with Your praise
And with Your glory all the day.   Ps. 71:8

Pause here to express any thoughts of adoration.

Prayers for Forgiveness

No temptation has overtaken you except such as is
common to man; but God is faithful, who will not
allow you to be tempted beyond what you are able,
but with the temptation will also make the way of
escape, that you may be able to bear it.

1 Cor. 10:13

If anyone sins, we have an Advocate with the Father, Jesus Christ the righteous. And He Himself is the propitiation for our sins, and not for ours only but also for the whole world. 1 John 2:1, 2

Pause here to ask the Spirit of God to bring to your mind specific sins for which you need forgiveness, and confess them to the Lord.

Prayers for Renewal

Grant that I may clothe myself with humility toward others, for
You resist the proud,
But give grace to the humble.

Therefore, may I humble myself under Your mighty hand that You may exalt me in due time, casting all my care upon You, because You care for me.
1 Pet. 5:5-7

May I be filled with the knowledge of Your will in all wisdom and spiritual understanding; that I may walk worthy of You, fully pleasing You, being fruitful in every good work and increasing in the knowledge of God; strengthened with all might, according to Your glorious power, for all patience and longsuffering with joy; giving thanks to the Father who has qualified me to partake of the inheritance of the saints in the light. Col. 1:9-12

Pause here for any additional prayers for renewal.

Prayers for Personal Needs

Relationships with Others
   Greater love and compassion for others
      Loved ones
      The lost
      Those in need
Special Concerns
My Activities for This Day

Prayers for Others

Evangelism
   Friends
   Neighbors
   Associates
   Special opportunities

Prayers of Affirmation

And He said to me, "My grace is sufficient for you, for My strength is perfect in weakness." Therefore most gladly I will rather boast in my infirmities, that the power of Christ may rest upon me.

2 Cor. 12:9

But without faith it is impossible to please Him, for he who comes to God must believe that He is, and that He is a rewarder of those who diligently seek Him.

Heb. 11:6

Pause here to add any personal affirmations.

Prayers of Thanksgiving

Oh, give thanks to the LORD!
Call upon His name;
Make known His deeds among the peoples!
Sing to Him, sing psalms to Him;
Talk of all His wondrous works!
Glory in His holy name;
Let the hearts of those rejoice who seek the LORD!
Seek the LORD and His strength;
Seek His face evermore!
Remember His marvelous works which He has done,
His wonders, and the judgments of His mouth.

1 Chr. 16:8-12

*Pause here for any personal expressions of
thanksgiving.*

Closing Prayers

Grace, mercy, and peace from God the Father and the
Lord Jesus Christ our Savior.   Titus 1:4

Blessed be the LORD forevermore!
Amen and Amen.   Ps. 89:52

Memory Verse: Use the Memory Verse Guide on
  pages 141-72.

Day 26

Scripture Reading: Select your Scripture reading from
the Bible Reading Guide on pages 113-40.

Prayers of Adoration

Praise the LORD!
Oh, give thanks to the LORD, for He is good!
For His mercy endures forever.
Who can utter the mighty acts of the LORD?
Who can declare all His praise?   Ps. 106:1, 2

The LORD lives!
Blessed be my Rock!
Let the God of my salvation be exalted.
                                        Ps. 18:46

I will praise the LORD according to His
    righteousness,
And will sing praise to the name of the LORD Most
    High.   Ps. 7:17

Pause here to express any thoughts of adoration.

Prayers for Forgiveness

Lord, You have said:

But on this one will I look:
On him who is poor and of a contrite spirit,
And who trembles at My word.   Is. 66:2

Has the LORD as great delight in burnt offerings and
    sacrifices,
As in obeying the voice of the LORD?

Behold, to obey is better than sacrifice,
And to heed than the fat of rams.   1 Sam. 15:22

The sacrifices of God are a broken spirit,
A broken and a contrite heart—
These, O God, You will not despise.   Ps. 51:17

*Pause here to ask the Spirit of God to bring to your
mind specific sins for which you need forgiveness,
and confess them to the Lord.*

Prayers for Renewal

Lord, You have said:

Hear, O Israel: The LORD our God, the LORD is one!
You shall love the LORD your God with all your heart,
with all your soul, and with all your strength.
                                        Deut. 6:4, 5

May I love You with all my heart, soul, and strength.

Father, according to Your Word:

May I have no other gods before You.
May I not make for myself [an idol].
May I not take Your name in vain.
May I remember the Sabbath day, to keep it holy.
May I honor my father and my mother.
May I not murder.
May I not commit adultery.
May I not steal.
May I not bear false witness against my neighbor.
May I not covet my neighbor's possessions.
                                        Ex. 20:3-17

Pause here for any additional prayers for renewal.

278

Prayers for Personal Needs

Faithfulness as a Steward
   With my time
   With my talents
   With my treasure
Special Concerns
My Activities for This Day

Prayers for Others

Government
   Revival
   Local government
   State government
   National government
   Current events and concerns

Prayers of Affirmation

Yes, if you cry out for discernment,
And lift up your voice for understanding,
If you seek her as silver,
And search for her as for hidden treasures;
Then you will understand the fear of the LORD,
And find the knowledge of God.
For the LORD gives wisdom;
From His mouth come knowledge and understanding;
He stores up sound wisdom for the upright;
He is a shield to those who walk uprightly.

Prov. 2:3-7

Pause here to add any personal affirmations.

Prayers of Thanksgiving

We give thanks to You, O God, we give thanks!
For Your wondrous works declare that Your name is
    near.   Ps. 75:1

The righteous shall be glad in the LORD, and trust in
    Him.
And all the upright in heart shall glory.   Ps. 64:10

*Pause here for any personal expressions of
thanksgiving.*

Closing Prayer

Now to Him who is able to keep us from stumbling,
And to present us faultless
Before the presence of His glory with exceeding joy,
To God our Savior,
Who alone is wise,
Be glory and majesty,
Dominion and power,
Both now and forever.
Amen.   Jude 24, 25

Memory Verse: Use the Memory Verse Guide on
    pages 141-72.

Day 27

Scripture Reading: Select your Scripture reading from the Bible Reading Guide on pages 113-40.

Prayers of Adoration

O God, my heart is steadfast;
I will sing and give praise, even with my glory.
Awake, lute and harp!
I will awaken the dawn.
I will praise You, O Lord, among the peoples,
And I will sing praises to You among the nations.
For Your mercy is great above the heavens,
And Your truth reaches to the clouds.
Be exalted, O God, above the heavens,
And Your glory above all the earth.   Ps. 108:1-5

Pause here to express any thoughts of adoration.

Prayers for Forgiveness

"Come now, and let us reason together,"
Says the Lord,
"Though your sins are like scarlet,
They shall be as white as snow;
Though they are red like crimson,
They shall be as wool."   Is. 1:18

Sing praise to the Lord, you saints of His,
And give thanks at the remembrance of His holy
    name.

For His anger is but for a moment,
His favor is for life;
Weeping may endure for a night,
But joy comes in the morning.   Ps. 30:4, 5

*Pause here to ask the Spirit of God to bring to your
mind specific sins for which you need forgiveness,
and confess them to the Lord.*

Prayers for Renewal

May I take up the whole armor of God, that I may be
able to withstand in the evil day, and having done all,
to stand. May I stand therefore, having girded my
waist with truth, having put on the breastplate of
righteousness, and having shod my feet with the
preparation of the gospel of peace; above all, taking
the shield of faith with which I will be able to quench
all the fiery darts of the wicked one. And may I take
the helmet of salvation, and the sword of the Spirit,
which is the word of God; praying always with all
prayer and supplication in the Spirit, being watchful
to this end with all perseverance and supplication for
all the saints.   Eph. 6:13-18

Lord, may I be clothed with Your armor.

Pause here for any additional prayers for renewal.

Prayers for Personal Needs

The Lord's Blessing and Enablement in My Roles
    Family
    Ministry

Evangelism
Discovery, development, and use of spiritual gifts
Career
Special Concerns
My Activities for This Day

Prayers for Others

Missions
Local missions
National missions
World missions
The fulfillment of the Great Commission
Special concerns

Prayers of Affirmation

"Not by might nor by power, but by My Spirit,"
Says the LORD of hosts. Zech. 4:6

The fear of the LORD is the beginning of wisdom,
And the knowledge of the Holy One is understanding.
Prov. 9:10

Pause here to add any personal affirmations.

Prayers of Thanksgiving

I will extol You, O LORD, for You have lifted me up,
And have not let my foes rejoice over me.
O LORD my God, I cried out to You,
And You healed me. Ps. 30:1, 2

*Pause here for any personal expressions of
thanksgiving.*

Closing Prayer

Oh, satisfy us early with Your mercy,
That we may rejoice and be glad all our days!

Ps. 90:14

Memory Verse: Use the Memory Verse Guide on
   pages 141-72.

Day 28

Scripture Reading: Select your Scripture reading from
the Bible Reading Guide on pages 113-40.

Prayers of Adoration

Oh, give thanks to the LORD!
Call upon His name;
Make known His deeds among the peoples!
Sing to Him, sing psalms to Him;
Talk of all His wondrous works!
Glory in His holy name;
Let the hearts of those rejoice who seek the LORD!
Seek the LORD and His strength;
Seek His face evermore!
Remember His marvelous works which He has done,
His wonders, and the judgments of His mouth.

Ps. 105:1-5

Be exalted, O LORD, in Your own strength!
We will sing and praise Your power. Ps. 21:13

Pause here to express any thoughts of adoration.

Prayers for Forgiveness

But He was wounded for our transgressions,
He was bruised for our iniquities;
The chastisement for our peace was upon Him,
And by His stripes we are healed.
All we like sheep have gone astray;
We have turned, every one, to his own way;
And the LORD has laid on Him the iniquity of us all.

Is. 53:5, 6

"Now, therefore," says the LORD,
"Turn to Me with all your heart,
With fasting, with weeping, and with mourning."
So rend your heart, and not your garments;
Return to the LORD your God,
For He is gracious and merciful,
Slow to anger, and of great kindness;
And He relents from doing harm.   Joel 2:12, 13

The LORD is near to those who have a broken heart,
And saves such as have a contrite spirit.

Ps. 34:18

*Pause here to ask the Spirit of God to bring to your
mind specific sins for which you need forgiveness,
and confess them to the Lord.*

Prayers for Renewal

May my love abound still more and more in
knowledge and all discernment, that I may approve
the things that are excellent, that I may be sincere
and without offense till the day of Christ, being filled
with the fruits of righteousness which are by Jesus
Christ, to the glory and praise of God.

Phil. 1:9-11

I do not count myself to have apprehended; but one
thing I do, forgetting those things which are behind
and reaching forward to those things which are
ahead, I press toward the goal for the prize of the
upward call of God in Christ Jesus.   Phil. 3:13, 14

Pause here for any additional prayers for renewal.

286

Prayers for Personal Needs

Personal Concerns
   Spiritual victory
      Over the world
      Over the flesh
      Over the Devil
   Continuous growth as a person
   Personal discipline
   Physical health and strength
Special Concerns
My Activities for This Day

Prayers for Others

World Affairs
   The poor and hungry
   The oppressed and persecuted
   Those in authority
   Peace among nations
   Current events and concerns

Prayers of Affirmation

No temptation has overtaken us except such as is common to man; but God is faithful, who will not allow us to be tempted beyond what we are able, but with the temptation will also make the way of escape, that we may be able to bear it.

1 Cor. 10:13

Pause here to add any personal affirmations.

Prayers of Thanksgiving

Oh, love the LORD, all you His saints!
For the LORD preserves the faithful,

287

And fully repays the proud person.
Be of good courage,
And He shall strengthen your heart,
All you who hope in the LORD.   Ps. 31:23, 24

*Pause here for any personal expressions of
thanksgiving.*

Closing Prayer

Now may the God of peace who brought up our Lord
Jesus from the dead, that great Shepherd of the
sheep, through the blood of the everlasting
covenant, make us complete in every good work to
do His will, working in us what is well pleasing in
His sight, through Jesus Christ, to whom be glory
forever and ever. Amen.   Heb. 13:20, 21

Memory Verse: Use the Memory Verse Guide on
     pages 141-72.

Day 29

Scripture Reading: Select your Scripture reading from the Bible Reading Guide on pages 113-40.

Prayers of Adoration

You who love the LORD, hate evil!
He preserves the souls of His saints;
He delivers them out of the hand of the wicked.
Light is sown for the righteous,
And gladness for the upright in heart.
Rejoice in the LORD, you righteous,
And give thanks at the remembrance of His holy
    name.   Ps. 97:10-12

Be glad in the LORD and rejoice, you righteous;
And shout for joy, all you upright in heart!
                    Ps. 32:11

Pause here to express any thoughts of adoration.

Prayers for Forgiveness

Blessed is he whose transgression is forgiven,
Whose sin is covered.
Blessed is the man to whom the LORD does not
    impute iniquity,
And in whose spirit there is no deceit.
When I kept silent, my bones grew old
Through my groaning all the day long.
For day and night Your hand was heavy upon me;
My vitality was turned into the drought of summer.
I acknowledged my sin to You,

And my iniquity I have not hidden.
I said, "I will confess my transgressions to the
     LORD,"
And You forgave the iniquity of my sin.

Ps. 32:1-5

*Pause here to ask the Spirit of God to bring to your
mind specific sins for which you need forgiveness,
and confess them to the Lord.*

Prayers for Renewal

May I count all things loss for the excellence of the
knowledge of Christ Jesus my Lord, for whom I have
suffered the loss of all things, and count them as
rubbish, that I may gain Christ and be found in Him,
not having my own righteousness which is from the
law, but that which is through faith in Christ, the
righteousness which is from You by faith; that I may
know Him and the power of His resurrection, and the
fellowship of His sufferings, being conformed to His
death.

Phil. 3:8-10

May my faith, being much more precious than gold
that perishes, though it is tested by fire, be found to
praise, honor, and glory at the revelation of Jesus
Christ.

1 Pet. 1:7

Pause here for any additional prayers for renewal.

Prayers for Personal Needs

Spiritual Growth
   Sensitivity to sin

Greater love and commitment to the Lord
Special Concerns
My Activities for This Day

Prayers for Others

The Church and Other Ministries
   My local church
   Other churches
   Other Christian ministries
   Educational institutions
   Special concerns

Prayers of Affirmation

But this I say: He who sows sparingly will also reap sparingly, and he who sows bountifully will also reap bountifully. So let each one give as he purposes in his heart, not grudgingly or of necessity; for God loves a cheerful giver.   2 Cor. 9:6, 7

Pause here to add any personal affirmations.

Prayers of Thanksgiving

I will greatly rejoice in the LORD,
My soul shall be joyful in my God;
For He has clothed me with the garments of
    salvation,
He has covered me with the robe of righteousness,
As a bridegroom decks himself with ornaments,
And as a bride adorns herself with her jewels.

         Is. 61:10

Pause here for any personal expressions of thanksgiving.

Closing Prayer

May the God of all grace, who called us to His
eternal glory by Christ Jesus, after we have suffered
a while, perfect, establish, strengthen, and settle us.
To Him be the glory and the dominion forever and
ever. Amen.   1 Pet. 5:10, 11

Memory Verse: Use the Memory Verse Guide on
     pages 141-72.

Day 30

Scripture Reading: Select your Scripture reading from the Bible Reading Guide on pages 113-40.

Prayers of Adoration

LORD, You have been our dwelling place in all
    generations.
Before the mountains were brought forth,
Or ever You had formed the earth and the world,
Even from everlasting to everlasting, You are God.

Ps. 90:1, 2

Inasmuch as there is none like You, O LORD
(You are great, and Your name is great in might),
Who would not fear You, O King of the nations?
For this is Your rightful due,
For among all the wise men of the nations,
And in all their kingdoms,
There is none like You.

Jer. 10:6, 7

Pause here to express any thoughts of adoration.

Prayers for Forgiveness

May we seek You, LORD, while You may be found,
Call upon You while You are near.
Let the wicked forsake his way,
And the unrighteous man his thoughts;
Let him return to You, LORD,
And You will have mercy on him;
And to You, our God,
For You will abundantly pardon.

Is. 55:6, 7

The heart is deceitful above all things,
And desperately wicked;
Who can know it?
You, LORD, search the heart,
You test the mind,
Even to give every man according to his ways,
According to the fruit of his doings.   Jer. 17:9, 10

*Pause here to ask the Spirit of God to bring to your
mind specific sins for which you need forgiveness,
and confess them to the Lord.*

Prayers for Renewal

Therefore, as the elect of God, holy and beloved,
may I put on tender mercies, kindness, humility,
meekness, longsuffering; bearing with others and
forgiving others, if anyone has a complaint against
another; even as Christ forgave me, so I also must
do. But above all these things may I put on love,
which is the bond of perfection. And may the peace
of God rule in my heart, that I may be thankful. May
the word of Christ dwell in me richly in all wisdom,
teaching and admonishing others in psalms and
hymns and spiritual songs, singing with grace in my
heart to the Lord. And whatever I do in word or
deed, may I do all in the name of the Lord Jesus,
giving thanks to God the Father through Him.
                                        Col. 3:12-17

Pause here for any additional prayers for renewal.

Prayers for Personal Needs

Need for Wisdom
   Wisdom for living life
   Developing an eternal perspective
   Renewal of my mind
Special Concerns
My Activities for This Day

Prayers for Others

Family
   My immediate family
   My relatives
   The salvation of family members
   Special concerns

Prayers of Affirmation

Before I was afflicted I went astray,
But now I keep Your word.
It is good for me that I have been afflicted,
That I may learn Your statutes.
I know, O LORD, that Your judgments are right,
And that in faithfulness You have afflicted me.

Ps. 119:67, 71, 75

Pause here to add any personal affirmations.

Prayers of Thanksgiving

Sing to the LORD, all the earth;
Proclaim the good news of His salvation from day to
   day.
Declare His glory among the nations,
His wonders among all peoples.

For the LORD is great and greatly to be praised;
He is also to be feared above all gods.
For all the gods of the peoples are idols,
But the LORD made the heavens.
Honor and majesty are before Him,
Strength and gladness are in His place.

1 Chr. 16:23-27

*Pause here for any personal expressions of
thanksgiving.*

Closing Prayers

Let the words of my mouth and the meditation of my
    heart
Be acceptable in Your sight,
O LORD, my strength and my Redeemer.

Ps. 19:14

Now to Him who is able to do exceedingly abundantly
above all that we ask or think, according to the
power that works in us, to Him be glory in the
church by Christ Jesus to all generations, forever and
ever. Amen.   Eph. 3:20, 21

Memory Verse: Use the Memory Verse Guide on
    pages 141-72.

Day 31

Scripture Reading: Select your Scripture reading from
the Bible Reading Guide on pages 113-40.

Prayers of Adoration

Blessed are You, LORD God of Israel, our Father,
forever and ever.
Yours, O LORD, is the greatness,
The power and the glory,
For all that is in heaven and in earth is Yours;
Yours is the kingdom, O LORD,
And You are exalted as head over all.
Both riches and honor come from You,
And You reign over all.
In Your hand it is to make great
And to give strength to all.
Now therefore, our God,
We thank You
And praise Your glorious name.   1 Chr. 29:10-13

Pause here to express any thoughts of adoration.

Prayers for Forgiveness

You are merciful and gracious,
Slow to anger, and abounding in mercy.
You will not always strive with us,
Nor will You keep Your anger forever.
You have not dealt with us according to our sins,
Nor punished us according to our iniquities.
For as the heavens are high above the earth,
So great is Your mercy toward those who fear You;

As far as the east is from the west,
So far have You removed our transgressions from us.
As a father pities his children,
So the LORD pities those who fear Him.
For You know our frame;
You remember that we are dust.   Ps. 103:8-14

*Pause here to ask the Spirit of God to bring to your
mind specific sins for which you need forgiveness,
and confess them to the Lord.*

Prayers for Renewal

May I sanctify Christ as Lord in my heart, and
always be ready to give a defense to everyone who
asks me a reason for the hope that is in me, with
meekness and fear.   1 Pet. 3:15

Grant that I may walk in wisdom toward those who
are outside, redeeming the time. May my speech
always be with grace, seasoned with salt, that I may
know how I ought to answer each one.
                                      Col. 4:5, 6

May I lay aside every weight, and the sin which so
easily ensnares me, and may I run with endurance the
race that is set before me, looking unto Jesus, the
author and finisher of my faith, who for the joy that
was set before Him endured the cross, despising the
shame, and has sat down at the right hand of the
throne of God.   Heb. 12:1, 2

Pause here for any additional prayers for renewal.

Prayers for Personal Needs

Spiritual Insight
  Understanding and insight into the Word
  Understanding my identity in Christ
    Who I am
    Where I came from
    Why I am here
    Where I am going
  The leading of the Lord and insight into God's will
Special Concerns
My Activities for This Day

Prayers for Others

Believers
  Personal friends
  People in ministry
  Those around the world who are oppressed and in
    need
  Special concerns

Prayers of Affirmation

For it is the God who commanded light to shine out
of darkness, who has shone in our hearts to give the
light of the knowledge of the glory of God in the face
of Jesus Christ. But we have this treasure in earthen
vessels, that the excellence of the power may be of
God and not of us.   2 Cor. 4:6, 7

Pause here to add any personal affirmations.

Prayers of Thanksgiving

God is our refuge and strength,
A very present help in trouble.   Ps. 46:1

My heart rejoices in the LORD;
My horn is exalted in the LORD.
I smile at my enemies,
Because I rejoice in Your salvation.
No one is holy like the LORD,
For there is none besides You,
Nor is there any rock like our God.   1 Sam. 2:1, 2

Therefore by Him let us continually offer the sacrifice of praise to God, that is, the fruit of our lips, giving thanks to His name.   Heb. 13:15

Pause here for any personal expressions of thanksgiving.

Closing Prayers

The LORD bless you and keep you;
The LORD make His face shine upon you,
And be gracious to you;
The LORD lift up His countenance upon you,
And give you peace.   Num. 6:24-26

Now may the God of hope fill us with all joy and peace in believing, that we may abound in hope by the power of the Holy Spirit.   Rom. 15:13

Memory Verse: Use the Memory Verse Guide on pages 141-72.

Personal
Prayer
Pages